D0565611

IN A PINCH

Effortless Cooking for Today's Gourmet

Caren McSherry

Foreword by Rob Feenie

whitecap

Copyright © 2010 by Caren McSherry
Foreword copyright © 2010 by Rob Feenie
Whitecap Books

All rights reserved. No part of this publication may be reproduced, stored in
a retrieval system, or transmitted in any form or by any means, electronic,
mechanical, photocopying, recording, or otherwise, without the prior written
permission of the publisher. For more information contact Whitecap Books,
at 351 Lynn Avenue, North Vancouver, BC, Canada V7J 2C4.

The information in this book is true and complete to the best of the author's
knowledge. All recommendations are made without guarantee on the part
of the author or Whitecap Books Ltd. The author and publisher disclaim any
liability in connection with the use of this information.

Whitecap Books is known for its expertise in the cookbook market, and has
produced some of the most innovative and familiar titles found in kitchens
across North America. Visit our website at www.whitecap.ca.

Edited by Melva McLean
Copy edited by Grace Yaginuma
Interior design by Working Format
Food photography by Hamid Attie
Food styling by Caren McSherry and Susan Meister

The recipes *Anna Olson's Rockwell Bake* (page 105) and *Chef Michael Smith's Penne
with Smoked Salmon and Cream Cheese Sauce* (page 96) have been reprinted with
permission from the authors.

This book is set in the typefaces Charlie (designed by Ross Milne) and
National (designed by Kris Sowersby).

Printed in Canada at Friesens

Library and Archives Canada Cataloguing in Publication

McSherry, Caren, 1952–
    In a pinch : effortless cooking for today's gourmet / Caren McSherry.

ISBN 978-1-77050-026-6

    1. Cooking. I. Title.

TX714.M362 2010   641.5   C2010-904637-4

The publisher acknowledges the financial support of the Government of
Canada through the Canada Book Fund (CBF) and the Province of British
Columbia through the Book Publishing Tax Credit.

10 11 12 13 14 5 4 3 2 1

ENVIRONMENTAL BENEFITS STATEMENT

Whitecap Books Ltd saved the following resources
by printing the pages of this book on chlorine free
paper made with 10% post-consumer waste.

TREES	WATER	SOLID WASTE	GREENHOUSE GASES
13	**6,010**	**365**	**1,248**
FULLY GROWN	GALLONS	POUNDS	POUNDS

Calculations based on research by Environmental Defense and the Paper Task Force.
Manufactured at Friesens Corporation

Contents

Features

Foreword

Caren is one damn good chef. She cooks from the heart, and anyone who knows her knows this: the most important ingredient in her recipes is love.

Caren and I have known each other for almost 20 years. I first met Caren when I was just a puppy in the restaurant biz, working alongside Michel Jacob at the fabulous Le Crocodile in Vancouver where she was a regular. I can still say I have never met anyone with as much energy and spirit as Caren. Every day she wears a huge smile, and her genuine enthusiasm for life is contagious.

Now, when you meet someone at Le Crocodile, it means they're serious about food—so that was one thing I knew about her. What I didn't know was that Caren was running both an amazing cooking school and a gourmet grocery store. The Gourmet Warehouse is a place that carries products no one else has in Vancouver. My wife has been buying treats for me for years from there, and she *still* finds things that surprise me. I also shop there for the Cactus Club Cafe. Over the years, I have also had the pleasure of leading several cooking demos at the store. Caren's cooking classes were always full of friends, both hers and mine, and they were full of Caren's contagious energy. They remain some of my best memories to this day.

I also have Caren to thank for introducing me to two of the most special people I know—Gary and Susie Meister. Since they are the godparents of my son, Devon, *and* the godparents of Caren's two gems, Christina and Jason, Caren and I have now in a way become family. Susie and Caren are great friends, great chefs, and amazing women, and I can tell you that makes for some great parties with some first-class food.

There are so many simple, fantastic recipes here, I'm not sure where to tell you to start! Maybe with the coconut prawns with plum dipping sauce…reading the recipe makes my mouth water. Or perhaps with the barbecued duck pizza (something my kids love) or with chicken pot pie (one of my faves). And I must mention two of my favourite sides: her spicy green beans and the Gruyère potatoes. Caren has knocked them out of the park!

Best of all, Caren really does show you how to make amazing food "in a pinch." But more importantly, she shows you how to have fun, enjoy yourself, and always remember: "It's just food!"

With all my love to Caren, and to all of Caren's readers—enjoy.

Rob Feenie
Food concept architect at the Cactus Club Cafe

For my two children, Christina and Jason,
my two gifts whom I hold very dear
Thank you for your patience and your love

My love of cooking began long ago—in Home Economics 10 at Templeton High, to be exact. Over the years, my affair with food has just grown more passionate and, at times, obsessive.

In the 80s, I was one of those cooking junkies who would spend three days preparing for a dinner party. The preparations routinely involved multiple-page recipes with several cross-referenced subrecipes and techniques that only the 80s equivalent of Iron Chef would attempt. I fretted about the perfection of carefully crafted butter balls or the size of lemon slices frozen and centered perfectly inside ice cubes. Multiple courses were the norm, with flatware laid out like tin soldiers along both sides of the matching charger plate. Napkins were persuaded into resembling birds, flowers, and bowties. Dinner parties were not carefree and casual; you *never* showed up in jeans, not even if they were Calvin's.

Fast forward to 2010…

Today, most of us have no idea what will unfold in the next two days, never mind two weeks. It's the "live for the moment" times, and we embrace it. As for the dinner party, we have totally re-invented it, for now and forever. Random, last-minute invites are common, not considered remotely rude, and not assumed to be a fill-in for a cancellation. We leap at opportunities to share a pot of chili, soup, or grilled fish and a bottle of wine. We hang out in the kitchen and belly up to the island, with the willingness to dig in and help—formalities be gone. Everyone pitches in, clears the table, and becomes thankful for the time together, whatever the format.

It's about the pleasure of friends and company. Midweek dinner invites have become the norm. I generally have friends over at least twice a week, and an extra friend is always welcome. It's great to rediscover the spirit of spontaneity. We all just show up and have fun!

I will confess to cheating my way around the kitchen on more occasions than one. Gone are the days of carefully measuring each of 12 spices that a homemade curry blend commands, or taking the time to work out the perfect flavors in a Moroccan rub. Instead, I now just *buy* them ready made. I have armed my pantry with the best rubs and spice mixtures the world has to offer.

This is one of my secret weapons: to enlist the premade by the dozens—a rub, a tapenade, a raspberry chipotle sauce, an onion jam, a beautiful lemon curd imported from Britain—to stand beside me in the kitchen as my sous chefs to aid in bringing the bold, bright flavors of my favorite dishes directly into my kitchen. Don't feel guilty about using good products that are available in gourmet stores and taking the shortcuts offered. These shortcuts do not minimize in any way your abilities as a cook; it does, however, maximize your time, relieve pressure, and allow you the joy to entertain with ease. Ban the formal, fancy settings and attitudes and embrace casual, easy entertaining. Who needs recipes that require multiple days of prep, or those themed parties that require a week's training with Martha and a budget to match?

The most important thing is to have a good time. It's just food!

The In a Pinch Pantry

Different lifestyles make it hard for me to suggest what you should have in your pantry. A lot depends on income and, these days, space, but this basic range of essentials should help you produce a few quick and simple dishes, including many in this cookbook. If you have more space available, assemble a pantry of some really delicious and interesting ingredients for everyday meals and a few special items to keep in reserve for impromptu entertaining.

Balsamic vinegar

By now, we all have a general understanding of this luscious condiment whose origins are firmly rooted in the Reggio Emilia region of Italy. Generally speaking, the older the better—but of course, the older it is, the more expensive it is. Pick a good 8-, 10-, or 12-year-old balsamic vinegar for special salads. Use the young, more affordable stuff for sauces and marinades.

Balsamic glaze is all the rage right now. You can easily make your own by boiling down a bottle of inexpensive vinegar. Go to page 157 to see how easy it is!

Other vinegars

Gone are the days when the pantry hosted just a basic red and a basic white wine vinegar. Neither provided much of an interesting profile to salad dressings anyway. Today, you can find so many varieties that you can just pick and choose your favorites. Besides balsamic (of course), there's fig, pear, tarragon, and even pecan vinegar in my pantry, and these are just a few of what I have. They last forever, and it's a nice little luxury to have so many varieties at my disposal.

Beans

Two choices here: dried or canned. Obviously, when I'm in a pinch, I always use canned beans. With dry, you have to plan ahead and factor in the soaking *and* cooking time. There are several recipes in the following pages that call for beans, and I suggest the canned variety to save you time.

Black pepper

Pepper is an integral ingredient in cooking. The best pepper in the world hails from India. Actually, India is famous for two kinds: Malabar and Tellicherry. Tellicherry is a bit more expensive because it's left on the vine longer in order to produce a larger corn. Both are great choices, and a little goes a long way when you use really good pepper.

Butter

Salted butter is more popular by far, but *unsalted* is what I prefer for all of my baking and cooking. I think the flavor is more honest, without the salt getting in the way, leaving it up to you to salt the dish as you wish. It is most often sold frozen.

Chili paste and chili sauce

I use these in my stir-frys and pasta sauces when I want a hit of hot. There are several on the market to choose from—sweet Thai, spicy Asian, Indonesian sambal. Where to start? Basically you really only need two— sweet and hot. So get a chili paste that leans on the sweet side so that you can serve it as is with wok-fried chicken or as an accent in a dipping sauce. Thai sauces tend to be on the sweet side. Then get a hot one—just a little goes a long way. I like to support local food champions instead of the huge multinationals, and Sisters Secret is one of these. The company is owned by a local B.C. girl who has great products.

Chipotle chilies

These are actually jalapeño peppers that are smoked over a wood fire in order to achieve their characteristic intense, smoky flavor. Chipotles have a good kick to them, so use with caution. They are sold in small cans packed in a sauce called adobo. I generally use just the pepper, leaving the sauce behind. There is no way you can use the entire can unless you are feeding a crowd of 50, so place the unused peppers in a Ziploc bag, flatten, and freeze. The next time a recipe calls for a chipotle, simply break a piece off from the frozen block.

Chocolate

Percentages, cocoa butter content, flavor profiles, origins—all of these details can actually make you crazy. The most important thing is to choose a good producer like Callebaut, Cacao Barry, or Valrhona. If a nut-free facility is important for you, Guittard is your chocolate. Quality will make all the difference in your desserts.

Figs

Figs have gone from being a virtual obscurity to a runaway success in a matter of a few years. One would rarely find them in produce stores, but they could always be found in abundance in the backyard gardens of families with European roots. My fortune has been always having these families as neighbors! Luckily now for all of us, when figs are in season, they are available everywhere. And dried figs—the plump Black Mission or Calimyrna varieties—are in supermarkets year round.

Grapeseed oil

I tend to use olive oil in most of my cooking, but there are dishes that require you to use a neutral oil to avoid competing with the flavors of the dish. Most South Asian and Indian foods require a neutral oil in order for their distinctive spices to shine. Peanut oil is an alternative but is considerably more pricey. Grapeseed oil is also very good for frying, as its smoke point is much higher than that of olive or vegetable oil.

Preserved lemon

This is one of the most essential ingredients in Middle Eastern/Persian cooking. It is simply whole lemons preserved in a brine of water, sugar, and salt, all of which infuse the lemons with a very distinct flavor. Salty, sweet, and sour would sum it up. Be aware that you only ever use the rind. Discard the soft pulpy inside and chop the rind as directed in the recipe.

Rubs

Ten years ago, you could pretty much sum up a rub as a salt and pepper coating on meat or chicken. It was more about sauces back in the day. As the quality of our cooking embellishments has improved, rubs have stepped in with layers of flavor. The choices are wide and varied from spicy to sweet, Indian to Mexican, and crisp crust finishes to brined infusions. Keeping rubs in the kitchen removes the worry and guesswork—no more blending select spices to achieve a specific flavor. I like to have several on hand—a Moroccan rub, a barbecue rub, and rubs made specifically for fish, lamb, and veggies. Use a different rub to switch up the same recipe.

Salt

Kosher, Murray River, *sel gris*, *fleur de sel*, Himalayan, Maldon—the origins (and thus the choices) are endless. I always have at least three to four selections on hand to give that final touch to dishes just prior to serving. Make no mistake: not all salts are the same. I encourage you to experiment—just don't oversalt.

Smoked Spanish paprika

This paprika should never be confused with or act as a substitute for Hungarian paprika. There is no close relationship or taste. Spanish paprika is from the Extremadura region of Spain. The peppers are oak smoked and dried, which gives a natural smokiness that is like no other. It is so prized that the Spanish government has given it a *Denominación de Origen*. Purchase it sweet, bittersweet, or hot.

Vanilla

Pods, extract, paste, or powder—whatever you choose, it is imperative that it be the real thing. No substitutes allowed! If you have room in your budget for only one choice, make it the paste. It is a thick, treasured mass of seeds and extract that will enhance any baking you do.

Appetizers

Mini Cheese Cones

Just when you think you've seen everything in food presentation, you turn a corner and discover something new and fantastic. I truly believe that is why we in the food world stay connected and excited. That's why I travel to all the great food shows on the planet. I discovered these tiny ice cream cones used for appetizers on my last trip to the New York Fancy Food Show.

Use dry lentils in a rimmed dish and stand the cones in them for a crowd-pleasing presentation. You can also use split peas, small beans, seeds—anything that will hold the cones upright. Be as creative as you like!

Makes 36

Place the cheese, butter, and paprika in a mixing bowl. Whip with a mixer for about 3 minutes until the mixture is smooth and creamy. Place the mixture in a piping bag fitted with a star tip; #16 is a good size.

Pour the dried lentils into a rimmed serving dish. Pipe the cheese mixture into the cones and garnish each with chopped toasted pistachio nuts. Stand them into the lentil dish and serve.

- 8 oz (250 g) cheddar spread (I use Imperial in the red tub)
- 6 Tbsp (90 mL) unsalted butter, softened
- 2 heaping Tbsp (30 mL+) smoked Spanish paprika
- 3 cups (750 mL) colorful dried lentils (to hold the cones)
- 36 mini cones (available at good gourmet stores)
- 36 shelled pistachio nuts, toasted and chopped (garnish)

IN A PINCH

If you can't find mini ice cream cones, use the smallest ones available at your local grocery store.

Blue Cheese and Caramelized Onion Dip

My good friend, and long-time sous chef at our cooking school, Doreen Corday, has graciously provided the recipe for this delicious dip. It truly is worth crying over the onions. One of those "take it away before I eat any more" dips that go great with chips, flatbread, and veggies. You can make this dip two days ahead and keep it refrigerated until the night of your party.

Makes 2 cups (500 mL)

Heat the oil in a medium frying pan; add the onion and cook, stirring occasionally, for about 20 minutes until golden brown. Sprinkle in the sugar to encourage browning. Remove from the heat when the onions are evenly caramelized. Cool completely.

Whisk the mayonnaise and sour cream together in a medium bowl. Add the blue cheese, and, using a spatula, mash till smooth. Stir in the caramelized onions. Season with pepper to taste.

Cover dip and refrigerate until flavors blend, at least 2 hours.

- 1 Tbsp (15 mL) olive oil
- 1¼ cups (310 mL) thinly sliced onion
- 1 Tbsp (15 mL) sugar
- ¾ cup (185 mL) mayonnaise
- ¾ cup (185 mL) sour cream
- 4 oz (125 g) blue cheese, softened
- Freshly ground pepper

IN A PINCH

Use leftover dip as a sauce for freshly cooked pasta.

Porcini Truffle Pâté

This supereasy pâté uses chicken livers as the base, with porcini powder infusing it with flavor. You can use jarred truffle slices; however, if this is not in your budget, a small drop of truffle oil will offer the essence of truffle at a fraction of the cost.

Makes 1 pound (500 g)

Place the butter in a nonstick frying pan over medium heat. Add the onion and cook for about 2 minutes to soften. Add the bacon and cook for about 5 minutes. Add the livers and sauté until they are just barely cooked. Set aside.

Line an 8½- × 4½-inch (1.5 L) loaf pan with the eight slices of bacon, letting them overlap, with the ends falling over the sides. Set the pan aside.

Transfer the cooked liver mixture to a food processor. Purée until smooth. Add the porcini powder and the brandy along with a good grinding of pepper to taste.

Pour the liver purée into the prepared pan. Line the top of the pâté with the bay leaves. Bring the overlapping bacon up and over to cover the bay leaves and enclose the pâté. Place the loaf in a hot-water bath (bain marie) and bake for 90 minutes in a preheated 250°F (120°C) oven. Remove from the oven and cool completely.

When cool, remove the pâté from the mould, discarding the bacon and bay leaves. Scrape any visible fat from the pâté. Place the pâté in a piping bag and pipe into little appie spoons. Garnish with the truffle slices.

Serve with toast points and cornichons on the side.

- 6 Tbsp (90 mL) unsalted butter
- 1 medium Spanish onion, finely chopped
- 4 oz (125 g) streaky bacon, chopped
- 1 lb (500 g) chicken livers, rinsed
- 8 additional slices bacon (to line loaf pan)
- 1 Tbsp (15 mL) Italian porcini mushroom powder
- ¼ cup (60 mL) brandy
- Freshly ground Tellicherry (or black) pepper
- 10 bay leaves
- Small individual serving spoons
- Truffle slices (garnish)

IN A PINCH

If the individual appie spoons are just too much to tackle, simply transfer the pâté to a serving crock and let your guests just go for it.

You can make this pâté up to four days before serving.

Fresh Fig and Chèvre Rolls

Prosciutto is one of my favorite ingredients. Here, the combination of cream cheese and chèvre (goat cheese) filling makes this roll different yet still easy.

Makes 16

Combine the chèvre and cream cheese in a bowl; add the horseradish, stir well to combine, and set aside.

Trim the stem end of each fig. Cut each fig in half widthwise, then slice each half into four, so that you end up with eight thin wedges from each fig.

Remove the fat edges from the prosciutto. You will be using four slices at a time: carefully lay one slice on your work surface with the short end towards you; overlap the next by about ½ inch (1 cm), then continue with two more slices. Spread ¼ cup (60 mL) of the cheese mixture over the prosciutto slices, leaving one-third of each end without cheese. Lay the figs in one row on the cheese without any gaps. You will use about one fig per roll — that is, about eight pieces, depending on the size of the fig. Squeeze a small drizzle of the balsamic glaze over the figs. Tightly roll up cigar style. Repeat with the remaining prosciutto, cheese mixture, and figs to get four long rolls.

Slice each roll in half on the diagonal, then cut each half in half again for a total of 16 rolls. If you prefer smaller pieces, cut accordingly.

Arrange on your serving plate cut side up and finish with an extra drizzle of the balsamic glaze.

- 8 oz (250 g) chèvre
- 4 oz (125 g) cream cheese, softened
- 1 Tbsp (15 mL) creamy horseradish
- 4–6 plump fresh figs
- 16 slices prosciutto
- 2 Tbsp (30 mL) Balsamic Glaze (page 157)

IN A PINCH

Use peeled kiwi fruit cut into quarters lengthwise instead of figs in this recipe.

Quick Appetizer Pizzas

There are moments when the thought of preparing dinner—with appies, yet—is overwhelming. When you're in a pinch, it helps to have store-bought flour tortillas on hand. They're perfect for quick and easy quesadillas and for this amazing pizza, which you can make in a frying pan or on a barbecue. The fig and ginger jam gives it an extra zing.

Serves 6 to 8

Lay the flour tortillas on your work surface. Spread each with Boursin cheese, jam, tapenade, and then Jack cheese (or chèvre), in that order. Place on a medium-hot barbecue grill and cook with the lid down until the cheese is melted. Or, place in a nonstick frying pan; cook for 2 minutes to crisp the tortilla, and then place the lid on until the cheeses melt.

Slice into wedges and serve immediately.

- ▸ Four 8-inch (20 cm) flour tortillas
- ▸ 5 oz (150 g) Boursin cheese
- ▸ ½ cup (125 mL) fig and ginger jam
- ▸ 4 oz (125 g) jarred tapenade (I use Brickstone's garlic and shiitake mushroom)
- ▸ 1 cup (250 mL) grated Monterey Jack (or chèvre)

IN A PINCH

You can find fig and ginger jam in most gourmet shops. But cherry jam from your local supermarket is a great substitute.

There is a plethora of fantastic jarred tapenades available on the market. Not just olive, but mushroom, onion, red pepper, sun-dried tomato—the list is extensive. Just choose your favorite!

Crab "Tootsie" Rolls
with Sake Dipping Sauce

These little "Tootsie" rolls can also be made ahead, frozen, thawed out, and then reheated in a 350°F (180°C) oven on the evening of your party. You can use small shrimp in place of the crab, or leave it out altogether and make this vegetarian.

Makes 18

For the dipping sauce, mix all the ingredients together in a small pot and simmer on low heat, whisking until the honey melts and the sauce is smooth. Remove from the heat and cool.

Place the cream cheese in a large bowl; add the crab, chives, cilantro, garlic, ginger, hoisin, sesame oil, and chili paste (if using). Mix well to ensure ingredients are evenly combined. Chill for about 15 minutes.

Lay a wrapper on your work surface. Place about 2 Tbsp (30 mL) of filling on the wrapper and, using your hands, roll the filling into a small log shape. Brush the edges of the wrapper with the beaten egg white, and roll up around the filling, closing in the ends. Repeat with remaining wrappers.

Fill a high-sided 8-inch (20 cm) nonstick frying pan with the grapeseed oil so that the oil comes up about an inch (2.5 cm). Heat the oil to 400°F (200°C). Drop the rolls into the hot oil and deep-fry until they turn golden brown— about 3 minutes. Drain on paper towels to absorb any excess oil. Serve with dipping sauce.

Sake Dipping Sauce

▸ ¼ cup (60 mL) sake
▸ 2 Tbsp (30 mL) rice vinegar
▸ 2 Tbsp (30 mL) liquid honey
▸ 2 Tbsp (30 mL) Dijon mustard
▸ 2 tsp (10 mL) wasabi powder (optional)

Rolls

▸ One 8 oz (250 g) pkg light cream cheese, softened
▸ ½ lb (250 g) fresh crabmeat, shredded
▸ 1 Tbsp (15 mL) snipped chives
▸ 2 Tbsp (30 mL) chopped fresh cilantro
▸ 1 clove garlic, minced
▸ 2 tsp (10 mL) freshly minced ginger
▸ 1 Tbsp (15 mL) hoisin sauce
▸ 1 Tbsp (15 mL) toasted sesame oil
▸ 1 tsp (5 mL) chili paste (optional)
▸ 18 thin egg roll wrappers
▸ 1 egg white, lightly beaten
▸ 1 cup (250 mL) grapeseed oil for frying

Crisp Guacamole Rolls

I love avocados and anything that goes with them. My daughter, Christina, shares the same love, and she makes one damn good guac. I am thrilled that she has become a truly good cook and shoves me aside when it comes to making guacamole. This recipe is for her, even if she never wants to be a chef!

Makes 24

Cut each Roma tomato in half; squeeze out the juice and dice. Place in a medium bowl with mashed avocado, shallots, garlic, lemon (or lime) juice, Worcestershire sauce, hot sauce, and cilantro. Mix well; add the salt to taste if you need to. Set aside.

Cut circles from the tortillas with the cookie cutter. (You should get three circles from each tortilla.) Lay the circles on your work surface; very lightly oil one side of the circle. Lay the oiled side down, place 1 Tbsp (15 mL) of guacamole down the middle, and tightly roll up the circle cigarlike. Place the tortilla circles seam side down on a very lightly oiled baking sheet, keeping the rolls resting against each other to prevent them from opening.

Bake in a preheated 400°F (200°C) oven for about 8 minutes; roll over and bake for another 2 minutes until tortilla circles are crisp. Transfer the rolls to a serving plate and let cool to room temperature.

Serve with an accent of your favorite prepared salsa.

- 2 large Roma tomatoes
- 2 ripe avocados, peeled and coarsely mashed
- 2 shallots, finely diced
- 1 large clove garlic, minced
- 2 Tbsp (30 mL) fresh lemon juice (or 1 Tbsp (15 mL) fresh lime juice)
- Good dash of Worcestershire sauce
- Good dash of your favorite hot sauce, or to taste
- ½ cup (125 mL) chopped fresh cilantro
- Sea salt
- Eight 8-inch (20 cm) flour tortillas
- 3-inch (8 cm) cookie cutter
- ¼ cup (60 mL) grapeseed oil

IN A PINCH

Use prepared guacamole to shorten up the prep time.

Tapenade Rolls

You'll never believe what you can do with a jar of tapenade and a loaf of sliced white. Who would have guessed? About the bread: don't get fancy —cheap sliced white is the bread of choice here.

Makes 24

Cut the crusts from the bread. With a rolling pin, flatten each bread slice so that it becomes as thin as possible. Spread 1 heaping Tbsp (15 mL+) of tapenade all over the slice and roll up jelly-roll fashion as tightly as possible. Place on a baking sheet seam side down. Brush the rolls all over with the melted butter.

Bake the rolls in a preheated 425°F (220°C) oven until they are golden brown. Remove and cut into half on the diagonal.

- ▸ 12 slices white bread (about ½ loaf)
- ▸ 1 cup (250 mL) jarred tapenade
- ▸ ½ cup (125 mL) melted unsalted butter

IN A PINCH

You can make the rolls two days in advance (do everything up to the brushing with butter) and chill (or freeze for up to three weeks). If freezing, thaw before baking.

Crab Avocado Stacks

Magical marriages in food do exist. Certain combinations of foods marry well: salmon and Pinot Noir, macaroni and cheese, and crab and avocado. For this appie, I actually use a healthy multigrain tortilla chip, an "antijunk snack food" that inspires me to take it beyond salsa.

This guacamole recipe is a bit different from the one I use for Crisp Guacamole Rolls (page 21). One less tomato makes this the perfect texture for baking on chips.

Makes 24

For the guacamole, cut the Roma tomato in half; squeeze out the juice and dice. Place in a medium bowl with mashed avocado, shallot, garlic, lemon juice, hot sauce, and Worcestershire sauce. Mix well; add the salt and pepper to taste if you need to. Set aside.

Choose chips that are completely whole and lay them on a baking sheet. Place 1 Tbsp (15 mL) of guacamole on each chip. Divide the crabmeat (or chicken) evenly among the chips. Top with the grated cheese.

Broil in a preheated oven until the cheese is melted and golden brown. Transfer to a colorful serving platter and enjoy.

IN A PINCH

Instead of making your own guacamole, use a convenient jar of guacamole seasoning to which you just add avocado!

Guacamole

- 1 large Roma tomato
- 2 ripe avocados, peeled and mashed
- 1 large shallot, minced
- 1 large clove garlic, minced
- 2 Tbsp (30 mL) fresh lemon juice
- 1–2 tsp (5–10 mL) your favorite hot sauce
- Dash of Worcestershire sauce
- Sea salt
- Freshly ground pepper

- 24 multigrain tortilla chips, kept whole
- 3½ oz (100 g) fresh crabmeat (or chicken), shredded
- 1 cup (250 mL) grated Monterey Jack

Coconut Prawns
with Plum Dipping Sauce

It's funny how often new creations are born from disaster. I was making this dish in one of my popular hors d'oeuvre cooking classes. Just as I was about to fry the prawns, the stovetop conked out. I had 25 students staring at me waiting to see how I would handle the problem. I calmly cranked the oven to high and baked them instead. The dish—and the class—was saved.

Makes 24

For the plum dipping sauce, place all the ingredients in a small stainless steel saucepan and warm just until the jam melts into liquid. Stir to combine and transfer to a serving bowl.

"Half-butterfly" the prawns, that is, butterfly them, but make sure the tail remains intact. Devein and drain-dry on paper towels.

Mix together the flour, cornstarch, salt, and pepper and place on a flat plate. Place the lightly beaten egg in one bowl and the coconut in the other. Dip each prawn into the egg, then the flour mixture, then the egg again, and finally the coconut. Place on a baking sheet until ready to deep-fry.

Fill a 10-inch (25 cm) high-sided nonstick frying pan with the grapeseed oil, which should come up about an inch (2.5 cm). Heat the oil until a small piece of bread dropped into it sizzles immediately. Gently drop the coated prawns into the oil, and cook for 2 to 3 minutes until the prawns are bright pink.

Serve with the plum dipping sauce.

Plum Dipping Sauce
- ¾ cup (185 mL) plum (or apricot) jam
- 2 Tbsp (30 mL) sweet chili sauce
- 1 Tbsp (15 mL) freshly grated ginger
- 1 tsp (5 mL) yuzu (or rice) vinegar
- 1 tsp (5 mL) fresh lime juice

Coconut Prawns
- 24 fresh prawns (26/30 count), peeled with tail left on
- 2 Tbsp (30 mL) unbleached all-purpose flour
- 2 Tbsp (30 mL) cornstarch
- ½ tsp (2 mL) sea salt
- ½ tsp (2 mL) freshly ground pepper
- 1 large egg, lightly beaten
- 1 cup (250 mL) flaked unsweetened coconut
- 2 cups (500 mL) grapeseed oil for frying

IN A PINCH

Instead of frying, you can bake these in a 400°F (200°C) oven. They're ready when they're bright pink.

Yuzu vinegar is a Japanese vinegar with overtones of lime, tangerine, and pine.

Stuffed Prawn Wontons with Grilled Pineapple Salsa

These prawn-stuffed wontons are a delicious appetizer.

Serves 6

For the salsa, heat the barbecue to medium-high. Lay the pineapple slices on the grill and brown evenly on both sides. Repeat with the onion, peppers, and whole jalapeño. Set aside the grilled fruit and vegetables to cool.

Once cool, evenly dice them and place in a bowl with the cilantro, mint, lime juice, and salt. Stir well to combine.

For the wonton filling, combine the lemongrass, garlic, ginger, and sweet chili sauce in a bowl. Season with the sea salt.

Cut the peeled prawns lengthwise down the back, taking care not to cut through and keeping the tail on. Open up and stuff about 1 tsp (5 mL) of the filling into each slit and press shut. Repeat, using all the prawns.

Lay the wonton wrappers on your work surface and cut each one in half on the diagonal to form a triangle. Brush with a small amount of sesame oil—just enough to moisten. Lay the stuffed prawn on top, allowing the tail to be jutting out from the cut side of the wonton wrapper. Wrap the prawn with the wonton wrapper.

Heat about ¼ inch (6 mm) of grapeseed oil in a shallow 10-inch (25 cm) frying pan. Fry the wrapped prawns about 1 minute each side until the wonton is golden and the prawn bright pink.

Remove from the pan and blot on paper towels to absorb any excess oil. While the wontons are still warm, roll them in the sesame seeds.

Serve on a platter with the pineapple salsa.

Pineapple Salsa

- 1 small pineapple, peeled, cored, and sliced
- 1 large onion, sliced
- 2 red peppers, cored and halved
- 1 whole jalapeño pepper (optional)
- ½ bunch fresh cilantro, roughly chopped
- ½ cup (125 mL) fresh mint leaves, chiffonade
- 2 tsp (10 mL) fresh lime juice
- Good pinch of Maldon or sea salt

Stuffed Prawn Wontons

- 2 stalks lemongrass (white part only), minced
- 2 cloves garlic, minced
- 2 Tbsp (30 mL) freshly minced ginger
- ½ tsp (2 mL) sweet chili sauce
- Pinch of sea salt
- 24 fresh prawns (26/30 count), peeled with tail left on
- 24 three-inch (8 cm) square wonton wrappers
- ⅓ cup (80 mL) toasted sesame oil
- Grapeseed oil for frying
- Toasted white sesame seeds (garnish)

IN A PINCH

Purchase peeled and cubed pineapple at your local grocery store and skip the grilling. Or just use a good jarred salsa instead of making your own!

Duck Taco Bites
with Chipotle Sauce

You don't have to tackle roasting a duck to make this easy recipe. Just purchase the roasted duck from your favorite Chinese takeout. Request that they split the duck in half; this makes the removal of the meat much easier. You can make these taco bites as large or as small as you like, depending on the size of cutter you use.

Makes 36

For the chipotle sauce, combine all the ingredients and transfer to a squeeze bottle. This sauce can be prepared and refrigerated up to four days ahead of time.

Cut the tortillas into 2-inch (5 cm) rounds using the cookie cutter. Heat grapeseed oil in a frying pan and fry the rounds in the hot oil; remove, and sprinkle with a pinch of sea salt. Set aside.

For the filling, heat the grapeseed oil in a large frying pan; add the onion and garlic and sauté until golden brown. Add the cabbage and cranberries and sauté until the moisture is gone. Add the shredded duck, cilantro, and water chestnuts. Toss to combine; season with sea salt and pepper to taste.

Heap the mixture onto the corn chip rounds, drizzle with the chipotle sauce, and top with toasted almonds.

IN A PINCH

A roasted supermarket rotisserie chicken is a good alternative to the roasted duck.

You can buy delicious flavored roasted almonds to use in the duck filling instead of plain toasted almonds. A good brand is Imperial Citrus Roasted Almonds from Nunes Farms.

Use a bag of store-bought corn tortilla chips instead of frying your own.

Chipotle Sauce
- 1 cup (250 mL) sour cream or crème fraîche
- 1 large chipotle pepper, finely chopped
- Squeeze of fresh lime juice
- Pinch of fleur de sel

Tortillas
- Twelve 8-inch (20 cm) soft corn tortillas
- 2-inch (5 cm) cookie cutter
- 3 Tbsp (45 mL) grapeseed oil for frying
- Sea salt for sprinkling

Filling
- ⅓ cup (80 mL) grapeseed oil
- 1 large sweet onion, sliced
- 2 cloves garlic, thinly sliced
- 3 cups (750 mL) shredded napa cabbage
- ⅔ cup (160 mL) dried cranberries
- 1 barbecued duck, skinned, boned, and shredded
- ½ cup (125 mL) chopped fresh cilantro
- 1 cup (250 mL) sliced water chestnuts
- Sea salt
- Freshly ground pepper
- 1 cup (250 mL) toasted almonds coarsely chopped

Grilled Asian Scallops with Chili Threads

A supersimple Asian marinade turns these scallops into a delicious appetizer. Make sure you use fermented black beans and not the black bean sauce.

Makes 36

For the marinade, heat the sesame oil and grapeseed oil together in a large saucepan; add the garlic, ginger, and chopped black beans. Sauté on medium heat until the mixture becomes fragrant, about 3 to 4 minutes. Add the rice vinegar and hoisin sauce. Stir to combine. Remove from the heat to cool.

Cut each scallop in half crosswise to get two rounds. Add to the cooled marinade and let them marinate for at least 30 minutes.

Heat a cast iron pan or a grill to high heat; sear the scallops on both sides for 3 to 4 minutes until cooked. Place one scallop on a decorative spoon (like a porcelain soup spoon) and garnish with the chili threads. Serve immediately.

- 2 Tbsp (30 mL) toasted sesame oil
- 2 Tbsp (30 mL) grapeseed oil
- 2 large cloves garlic, minced
- 1-inch (2.5 cm) piece fresh ginger, peeled and grated
- 1 Tbsp (15 mL) finely chopped fermented black beans
- 1 Tbsp (15 mL) rice vinegar
- 1 Tbsp (15 mL) hoisin sauce
- 18 large sea scallops
- Individual serving spoons
- Chili threads (garnish)

IN A PINCH

Chili threads, which can be found in good gourmet stores, are finely julienned pieces of chili that are dehydrated and hold just a hint of heat. They make a very sexy garnish.

If you don't have decorative serving spoons, pan-fry small slices of potato until golden brown on both sides. Blot excess oil and top with the cooked scallop.

Salmon Squares

The secret to making the squares square (or rectangles rectangular) is having the courage to aggressively trim the salmon side to a perfect rectangle to start with. It's sort of a "cheffy" thing to do to achieve The Look. Most home cooks shy away from any waste, but give it a try. Trim that side down and just get over it! You can always make a stir-fry with the ends.

Makes 24

Place the salmon on your work surface; trim the belly from the head end to the tail end in a straight line. Cut most of the tail end off, and square off the collar end. You should have a perfect rectangle. Slice into smaller squares or rectangles so that you end up with 24 pieces.

Pat the nonskin sides with the rub. The longer the rub sits on the salmon, the better, but in a pinch, you don't need to wait because the rub is flavorful enough.

Heat grapeseed oil in a nonstick pan, place the salmon pieces in the pan skin side down, and fry until pieces are just opaque in the middle.

Remove from the pan and place on a serving platter. Insert the forks into the centers and garnish the top with one whole cilantro (or chervil) leaf.

- ▸ 2 lb (1 kg) whole fillet of wild B.C. salmon
- ▸ ½ cup (125 mL) your favorite dry rub
- ▸ 1 Tbsp (15 mL) grapeseed oil for frying
- ▸ 24 flat-sided mini bamboo forks (two-pronged)
- ▸ 24 fresh cilantro (or chervil) leaves (garnish)

IN A PINCH

I like to experiment with different rubs, as there are so many choices available. I often mix and match up my collection of store-bought rubs, creating great spontaneous flavors. If you do this too, remember to jot down your personal concoctions, because you never know when you'll hit a home run in the kitchen.

Salmon Gyoza
with Ginger Soy Dipping Sauce

I prefer Indian candy—a sweet smoked salmon—from West Coast Select because the flavor is a crowd pleaser and the brand can be found in almost all supermarkets.

Makes 24

Combine all the ingredients for the dipping sauce in a bowl. Set aside.

Remove the skin from the Indian candy; pull apart the salmon until it is completely flaked. Place salmon and the remaining ingredients for the gyoza filling in a bowl; stir well to combine. Season with salt and pepper to taste.

Lay the wrappers on your work surface; place a spoonful of filling in the center of each. Brush the entire edge of the wrapper with water; fold over to create a sealed half moon. Press the edges with the tines of a fork to seal.

Heat a large saucepan to medium heat; add just enough grapeseed oil to coat the pan. Place the gyoza in a single layer and fry for 1 minute on each side until golden brown.

Drizzle about ½ cup (125 mL) of water overtop; cover and cook for 1 minute more. (The goal is to have a browned surface with a soft inside.)

Remove from the pan and serve with the ginger soy dipping sauce.

IN A PINCH

The gyoza can be assembled in advance and frozen. Make sure to thaw before frying to ensure they cook thoroughly.

Ginger Soy Dipping Sauce

- ½ cup (125 mL) soy sauce
- 2 Tbsp (30 mL) toasted sesame oil
- 2 tsp (10 mL) fish sauce
- 1 tsp (5 mL) freshly grated ginger
- 1 tsp (5 mL) sweet chili sauce (optional)

Salmon Gyoza

- 8 oz (250 g) Indian candy
- 1 cup (250 mL) sautéed shredded napa cabbage, drained of moisture
- ⅓ cup (80 mL) thinly sliced green onions
- ¼ cup (60 mL) finely chopped green pepper
- 3 Tbsp (45 mL) wasabi mayonnaise
- 2 Tbsp (30 mL) toasted sesame oil
- 2 Tbsp (30 mL) soy sauce
- 2 tsp (10 mL) freshly grated ginger
- Pinch of sea salt
- Freshly ground pepper
- 24 round wonton wrappers
- Grapeseed oil for frying

Curried Beef Wontons with Two Dipping Sauces

One of the reasons I really like this recipe is because you can make a double batch of wontons and freeze them, and that gives you the option of using them for predinner appies on a whim. You want the ground beef to be very finely minced. Ask your butcher to do this for you.

Makes 24 wontons

Place the ground beef in a large bowl and add all the remaining ingredients for the filling. Mix well to distribute the seasonings evenly.

Lay six wonton wrappers on your work surface; place a teaspoon or two (5–10 mL) of the filling in the center of the wrapper squares. Dip your fingers in water and moisten the edge of the wrappers.

Form the wontons into any shape you wish. You can gather all the edges together to make little pouches. Or fold the wrapper over to make a triangle, and then pinch the two opposite corners together. Place the finished wontons on a lightly cornstarch-dusted baking sheet and chill until ready to cook.

Fill a 10-inch (25 cm) high-sided nonstick frying pan with the grapeseed oil, which should come up about an inch (2.5 cm). Heat the oil until hot. Test the oil with a piece of wonton wrapper—if it browns immediately, proceed with frying the filled wontons in a single layer until they are golden brown. Remove and blot on paper towels to absorb excess oil.

Serve hot with the dipping sauces (facing page).

Filling

- 1 lb (500 g) finely minced extra-lean ground beef
- 2 large shallots, minced
- 3 large cloves garlic, minced
- 2 Tbsp (30 mL) toasted sesame oil
- 2 Tbsp (30 mL) good-quality curry powder
- 2 Tbsp (30 mL) freshly minced ginger
- 1 Tbsp (15 mL) soy sauce
- 2 tsp (10 mL) chili paste
- 2 tsp (10 mL) kosher salt
- 1 tsp (5 mL) freshly ground pepper
- 1 egg, beaten

- 24 three-inch (8 cm) square wonton wrappers
- 2 cups (500 mL) grapeseed (or vegetable) oil

IN A PINCH

Use a jarred honey mustard sauce instead of making your own; you will make a small sacrifice in flavor, but it is a time-saver!

If making ahead of time to freeze, follow recipe until wontons are ready to be fried. Freeze. When ready to use, defrost wontons and heat in a 350°F (180°C) oven for 10 minutes before frying.

Honey Mustard Sauce

Makes ¾ cup (185 mL)

- ▸ ½ cup (125 mL) grainy mustard
- ▸ ¼ cup (60 mL) sake or beer, plus more to thin sauce
- ▸ 2 Tbsp (30 mL) dried mustard
- ▸ 2 Tbsp (30 mL) liquid honey
- ▸ 1 Tbsp (15 mL) white wine (or rice) vinegar
- ▸ 1 tsp (5 mL) chili paste or flakes, or to taste

Combine all the ingredients in a medium saucepan and, maintaining the heat on low, whisk the sauce until it is smooth and has a dipping consistency. Thin with additional sake or beer, if necessary.

Lingonberry Ginger Sauce

Makes 1 cup (250 mL)

- ▸ 2 Tbsp (30 mL) balsamic vinegar
- ▸ 1 Tbsp (15 mL) white wine
- ▸ 1 shallot, minced
- ▸ 1 clove garlic, minced
- ▸ 2 tsp (10 mL) freshly minced ginger, or more to taste
- ▸ 1 cup (250 mL) lingonberries (jarred)
- ▸ Extra wine or water to thin sauce

Combine all the ingredients, except for lingonberries, in a small stainless steel pot. Bring to a slow simmer and then add the berries. Slowly heat sauce through, adjusting the consistency of the sauce with additional wine or water, if necessary.

Chicken Drummettes

These perfect two-bite appies work well in a pinch, like when you have to feed a large gathering at a minimal cost. Country ketchup is the name for upscale, gourmet-type ketchup. Use good old Heinz if you can't find the fancy-ass kind!

Makes 24

Mix all the ingredients, except the chicken, in a large bowl to make the marinade.

Cut through the middle of each drummette to expose the bone. Scrape your knife down the bone, pushing the meat to the bottom. Form a ball as you pull the meat down.

Place the drummettes in the marinade for at least 2 hours. Remove and transfer to a parchment-lined baking sheet. Bake in a preheated 375°F (190°C) oven for 1 hour.

Serve the drummettes hot or at room temperature.

- ½ cup (125 mL) country ketchup
- ⅓ cup (80 mL) Jack Daniel's bourbon (or rum or water)
- 2 Tbsp (30 mL) tamari soy sauce
- 2 Tbsp (30 mL) brown sugar
- 2 Tbsp (30 mL) granulated garlic (not garlic powder)
- 1 chipotle pepper, minced (less if you are timid)
- 24 chicken mini-drumsticks (see In a Pinch)

IN A PINCH

For easy cleanup, use Silpat baking sheets. They're good for about 3,000 uses, which makes them a great green alternative to parchment paper.

Whole chicken wings are usually sold separated into mini-drumsticks and mini-wings. Mini-drumsticks are sometimes referred to as *drummettes*, and they're the meaty section attached to the breast; mini-wings, aka *wingettes*, are the flat, middle portion of the wing, with two bones. You can also use wingettes in the recipe! Scrape your knife down the two bones, pushing the meat to the bottom. Snap off the thin bone and discard.

If the store sells only whole chicken wings, you'll have to split them yourself by cutting them in half where the drummette and wingette meet.

Purchase a good BBQ sauce or marinade to save time.

Mini Lamb Burgers

Sliders (aka mini burgers) have become an obsession in most hip bistros and bars. They are cute, taste great, and just slide down. Ground beef is a perfectly good alternative to ground lamb.

Makes 24

Combine the ground lamb with the rest of the ingredients for the patties in a large bowl and mix well. Form into 2-inch (5 cm) patties and pan-fry or barbecue on both sides until cooked through.

Toast the hamburger buns until lightly golden brown; spread both sides with a good smear of onion jam, and then top each patty with a handful of the arugula (or watercress) and a strip of fire-roasted red pepper. Sandwich it together, top with an olive, and skewer with a decorative pick. Serve warm.

IN A PINCH

Onion jam, which is available at most grocery stores, is just caramelized onions. It goes great on pizza, chicken breasts, and these little sliders.

The mini buns can be tricky to source, but many bakeries do make them to order. You can also punch out 2-inch (5 cm) circles from regular buns.

Burger Patties

- 1 lb (500 g) lean ground lamb
- ½ cup (125 mL) panko (Japanese breadcrumbs)
- ⅓ cup (80 mL) toasted pine nuts
- 2 Tbsp (30 mL) chopped preserved lemon
- ½ cup (125 mL) chopped fresh cilantro
- 2 shallots, finely chopped
- 2 cloves garlic, minced
- 2 tsp (10 mL) chopped jalapeño
- ½ tsp (2 mL) ground cinnamon
- ½ tsp (2 mL) ground cardamom
- ½ tsp (2 mL) sea salt
- 1 large egg, lightly beaten

- 24 mini burger buns
- 1 cup (250 mL) onion jam
- 1 heaping cup (250 mL+) arugula (or watercress)
- One 14 oz (398 mL) jar fire-roasted red peppers, blotted dry
- 24 pitted green olives
- 24 decorative cocktail picks

5 Quick & Easy Appetizers

1   **Artichoke dip**
Drain a 14 oz (398 mL) jar of marinated artichokes. Drain and rinse a 14 oz (398 mL) can of cannellini beans. Place both in the bowl of a food processor. Add 2 cloves of garlic, 1 Tbsp (15 mL) of your favorite dry rub, and 1 cup (250 mL) grated Parmesan cheese. Purée. (Add olive oil if you prefer a thinner dip.) Scrape down the bowl, season with kosher salt, and garnish with Italian parsley. Dip!

2   **Foie gras bites**
Place 7 oz (200 g) foie gras mousse in a mixing bowl. Beat in 2 Tbsp (30 mL) of softened unsalted butter until the mixture is light and fluffy. Mix in 1 Tbsp (15 mL) of balsamic glaze. (There are several kinds you can buy—I like to use *fig* balsamic glaze.) Transfer the mixture to a piping bag fitted with a star tip and pipe the mixture onto small circles of bread. Garnish each with a small piece of dried Black Mission fig.

3   **Prosciutto-wrapped bocconcini**
Wrap thin slices of Italian prosciutto around 1-inch (2.5 cm) balls of bocconcini. If you can't find the smaller balls, simply cut large balls of bocconcini cheese into quarters. (There's no need to skewer these—it all holds together well.) Grill wrapped cheese on the barbecue or pan-fry in a hot nonstick frying pan until the prosciutto is crisp. Serve hot.

4   **Stuffed mushrooms**
Mix a package of Boursin cheese with 1 cup (250 mL) of panko crumbs. Pull the stems from 18 medium-sized fresh white button mushrooms and stuff the cheese mixture into each cavity. Bake in a 375°F (190°C) oven for 10 minutes or until the mushrooms are soft but not soggy. You can also place them on a hot barbecue, a nice appetizer served right from the Q. Give each a good grind of pepper to finish.

5   **Tomato bites**
Cut the tops from 12 cherry tomatoes. Using a butter baller, scoop out and discard the pulp. Fill the cavity of each with pesto sauce or a jarred tapenade, and top with a toasted pine nut.

Soups & Salads

Roasted Butternut Squash
and Corn Soup

Soup is the heart and soul of comfort; just one big spoonful of homemade goodness makes all the stress of a day disappear. Make a double batch and freeze half to keep on hand for unexpected storms—be they weather or personal—or for impromptu midweek dinner parties.

Serves 6

Remove the husk and silk from the corn cobs. Cut the kernels off with a knife. Fry in a cast iron frying pan *without* oil or butter until corn is dark and roasted.

Cut each squash in half; scoop out and discard the seeds. Place 1 Tbsp (15 mL) butter in each of the four squash cavities. Season with sea salt and pepper to taste. Place squash halves on a baking sheet and roast in a preheated 350°F (180°C) oven for 45 minutes.

Heat the remaining 2 Tbsp (30 mL) butter and the oil in a large saucepan. Add the onion and sauté for 5 minutes. Stir in the garlic, ginger, curry powder, and ground cardamom and sauté for an additional 3 to 5 minutes.

Scoop out the cooked squash from each shell and add to the saucepan along with the chicken stock. Simmer for 15 minutes and then purée in small batches in a food processor, or with a stick blender, until the squash is smooth. (Be careful not to let the liquid splash onto you; it will be very hot.) When smooth, return soup to the pot and simmer for another 15 minutes.

To serve, ladle the soup into bowls, top with the roasted corn, then garnish with parsley, cilantro, and a dollop of sour cream (or crème fraîche or yogurt).

- 2 cobs fresh corn or one 14 oz (398 mL) can
- 2 medium butternut squashes
- 6 Tbsp (90 mL) unsalted butter, divided
- Sea salt
- Freshly ground pepper
- 2 Tbsp (30 mL) olive oil
- 1 large onion, sliced
- 1 large clove garlic, minced
- 1-inch (2.5 cm) piece fresh ginger, peeled and grated
- 2 Tbsp (30 mL) good-quality curry powder
- ½ tsp (2 mL) ground cardamom
- 8 cups (2 L) chicken stock
- ⅓ cup (80 mL) chopped parsley (garnish)
- ⅓ cup (80 mL) chopped fresh cilantro (garnish)
- ½ cup (125 mL) sour cream (or crème fraîche or yogurt) (garnish)

Roasted Cherry Tomato Gazpacho

Cold soup on a hot summer day is completely refreshing. I created this recipe by chance when I noticed that the grape tomatoes I had purchased a few days earlier were beginning to wither. I cut them in half and roasted them. The rest is recipe!

Serves 6

Cut the tomatoes in half and place skin side down in a single layer on an oiled baking sheet. Sprinkle with the sea salt, pepper, and chopped garlic, and drizzle with the olive oil. Roast in a preheated 350°F (180°C) oven for 20 to 30 minutes. Remove and cool.

When cool, place in a large bowl and add the Clamato and tomato juice, water, onion, cucumber, olives, horseradish, Worcestershire sauce, and sherry vinegar. Stir to mix well; chill for 2 hours or freeze for up to 2 days.

To serve, ladle the chilled soup into clear stemmed bowls or large wine glasses, top with the crumbled feta, and lay a cheese stick or a piece of bread on top of each bowl or glass.

IN A PINCH

Prepare this soup a few days ahead of a dinner party (when you have time) and chill until the big day. The flavors infuse during the chill, making the soup even better.

- 2 lb (1 kg) cherry (or grape) tomatoes
- ½ tsp (2 mL) sea salt
- Freshly ground Tellicherry (or black) pepper
- 2–3 large cloves garlic, finely chopped
- ½ cup (125 mL) olive oil
- 3 cups (750 mL) Clamato juice
- 2 cups (500 mL) tomato juice
- 1 cup (250 mL) water
- 1 large sweet onion, diced
- 1 small English cucumber, diced
- ⅔ cup (160 mL) green olives, pitted and chopped
- 1 Tbsp (15 mL) creamy horseradish
- 1 Tbsp (15 mL) Worcestershire sauce
- ¼ cup (60 mL) sherry vinegar
- Crumbled feta cheese (garnish)
- 6 Reggiano Cheese sticks (page 130) or 6 pieces flatbread, focaccia, or wide bruschetta

Christina's Simple Chunky Tomato Soup

Making your own tomato soup doesn't have to be labor intensive. My friend Susan Meister, the owner of Fabulous Foods Catering, is my daughter's godmother; Susan developed this recipe for Christina. You can whip it up in no time for a midweek or impromptu weekend dinner. To make this into a grown-up dinner-party soup, add ½ cup (125 mL) gin. Voilà!

Serves 4

Heat the olive oil in a stockpot over medium heat; sauté the onion and garlic until softened. (Don't let them brown!) Add the tomatoes and break them up with the back of a wooden spoon. There will still be some chunky pieces of tomato, but this adds character to the soup. (If you prefer a smoother texture, you can of course purée the soup at the end, after simmering.)

Pour in chicken stock and let the soup simmer for approximately 20 minutes. Add the basil and season to taste with sea salt and pepper. Drizzle each serving with balsamic glaze.

- 2 Tbsp (30 mL) olive oil
- 1 small yellow onion, finely chopped
- 1 large clove garlic, minced
- One 28 oz (796 mL) can whole San Marzano tomatoes
- ½ cup (125 mL) chicken stock
- ⅓ cup (80 mL) fresh basil leaves, julienned
- Sea salt
- Freshly ground pepper
- 2 Tbsp (30 mL) Balsamic Glaze (page 157)

IN A PINCH

San Marzano are a specific variety of Italian plum tomatoes that are robust and full of flavor and are much meatier in structure than beefsteak tomatoes. They are perfect for making soups and sauces.

Fennel Velouté with Shrimp

You can also serve this soup in espresso cups or small bowls. People will just love the presentation because it's so darn cute. In fact, there's no reason not to serve other soups like this!

Serves 8

Heat the oil and butter in a large stockpot; add the shallots and garlic, and sauté for about 5 minutes. (Do not brown!) Add the fennel and celery; cook, stirring, for an additional 6 to 10 minutes. Add the chicken stock and fresh thyme.

Simmer for about 20 minutes and then purée in small batches in a blender or food processor, or with a stick blender, until the fennel is smooth. (Be careful not to let the liquid splash onto you; it will be very hot.)

Strain and place soup back into the pot. Add the cream, parsley, chili flakes, and lime juice. Adjust the seasoning, if needed, with salt and pepper.

To serve, portion the soup. Thread three cooked shrimp on each skewer, sprinkle with a pinch of fleur de sel, and set one skewer in each cup.

IN A PINCH

You can usually find cooked, hand-peeled medium-sized shrimp (36/40 count) with the tails still on in the seafood section of your supermarket. They're very convenient and make for a great presentation as well!

- ¼ cup (60 mL) olive oil
- 2 Tbsp (30 mL) unsalted butter
- 4 large shallots, diced
- 2 cloves garlic, chopped
- 2 large bulbs fennel, cored and chopped
- 1 stalk celery, chopped
- 4 cups (1 L) chicken stock
- 3 sprigs fresh thyme, leaves only
- 1 cup (250 mL) half and half cream (10–12%)
- ¼ cup (60 mL) parsley leaves
- Pinch of chili flakes
- 1 Tbsp (15 mL) fresh lime juice
- Kosher salt
- Freshly ground pepper
- 8 mini skewers
- 24 shrimp (36/40 count), cooked and peeled
- Fleur de sel

Quick Bouillabaisse

This tomato-based seafood soup has its roots firmly planted in the south of France. Here on the West Coast, we have a terrific selection of fresh shellfish to choose from—enough to rival the likes of the French.

Serves 6

Heat the olive oil in a large 8-quart (9 L) stockpot. Add the onions, fennel slices, and garlic and sauté until lightly golden. Add the tomatoes, tomato sauce, red wine, paprika, and parsley. Bring the mixture to a boil; add the bay leaf, tarragon, salt, and pepper.

Place the crab legs in the pot, then add the halibut, mussels, clams, and prawns; cover and simmer for 10 to 15 minutes until the halibut is opaque. Discard any unopened mussels or clams.

To serve, distribute the fish among six bowls; ladle the stock overtop, and garnish with wedges of lemon, reserved fennel fronds, and aioli.

IN A PINCH

Garlic aioli or garlic mayo is easily purchased jarred and provides that little bit of zip. You can also make aioli from scratch if you have time (page 154).

The best time to purchase, eat, and cook fresh shellfish is during the months in the year that have the letter r in them because that's when the waters are the coldest and the shellfish is at its optimum flavor.

- ½ cup (125 mL) olive oil
- 2 medium yellow onions, diced
- 1 small bulb fennel, cored and thinly sliced (save the fronds)
- 3 large cloves garlic, chopped
- 5 large Roma tomatoes, diced
- Two 14 oz (398 mL) jars Italian tomato sauce
- 1 cup (250 mL) red wine
- 2 tsp (10 mL) smoked Spanish paprika
- ½ bunch Italian parsley, chopped
- 1 bay leaf
- 2 tsp (10 mL) dried tarragon
- 1 tsp (5 mL) sea salt
- 1 tsp (5 mL) freshly ground pepper
- 12 fresh Dungeness crab legs, cracked
- 1 lb (500 g) halibut fillets, cut into 2-inch (5 cm) cubes
- 24 fresh mussels, scrubbed and debearded
- 24 fresh littleneck (or cherrystone) clams, scrubbed
- 24 large fresh prawns (26/30 count), shells kept on, heads off (fresh or frozen)
- 2 lemons, cut into wedges (garnish)
- Fennel fronds (garnish)
- store-bought garlic aioli (or Simple Basil Aioli—page 154) (garnish)

Lemongrass Shrimp Soup

A perfect little soup for a first course: brimming over with flavor but not filling. And quick to prepare. You can use chicken as a substitute for the shrimp, or substitute 1 cup (250 mL) of shelled edamame for a vegetarian variation. This soup comes together so quickly, we could call it heat and serve, but that would sound terrible.

Serves 4 to 6

In a large pot, heat the stock, lime juice, fish sauce, lemongrass, lime leaves, ginger, and chili. Bring to a boil and simmer for about 5 minutes. Add the mushrooms and shrimp and cook for about 4 minutes until heated through, and the shrimp are bright pink.

Garnish with cilantro leaves and serve hot.

IN A PINCH

The quickest way to grate ginger without getting strings is to peel it, pop it into a Ziploc bag, and freeze it. When you need ginger, simply use a Microplane to grate the frozen ginger. It comes out string free and almost powderlike. Fantastic, I say!

- 5 cups (1.25 L) light fish stock, chicken stock, or vegetable stock
- ¼ cup (60 mL) fresh lime juice
- 2 Tbsp (30 mL) fish sauce
- Two 4-inch (10 cm) pieces lemongrass, sliced very thin
- 2 kaffir lime leaves, chiffonade
- 1 Tbsp (15 mL) freshly minced ginger
- 1 red chili, seeds removed and sliced very thin
- 1 cup (250 mL) enoki mushrooms (or fresh shiitake mushrooms, julienned)
- ½ lb (250 g) fresh shrimp, peeled
- ½ cup (125 mL) fresh cilantro leaves (garnish)

Filo-Wrapped Camembert on Spinach Salad

I like to wrap a piece of Camembert or brie in filo pastry, bake it, and then put it on top of a plate of spinach or mixed greens with a brilliant little dressing made from a jar of preserves. It's so easy and oh so good. Your guests will think you've been slaving in the kitchen for hours.

Serves 6

Lay one filo sheet on your work surface; brush lightly with the oil and fold it in half lengthwise. Cut the filo in half lengthwise. Do not unfold. You will have two long strips of layered filo, about 3 inches (7 cm) wide. Repeat with the next two sheets of filo.

Cut the cheese into six equal portions, leaving the rind on. Place one piece of the cheese on one end of the filo, and fold it up and over itself in a triangular shape to enclose the cheese entirely. Repeat so that you end up with six wrapped pieces.

Bake in a preheated 375°F (190°C) oven for about 10 minutes until the parcel is golden brown.

While the filo packets bake, heat the olive oil in a small saucepan; add the shallot and sauté until just soft. Add the preserves and brandy and heat through. Set aside.

To serve, place the spinach (or mixed greens) in a salad bowl. Lightly drizzle with good olive oil and a sprinkle of sea salt. Toss to coat. Divide the spinach among six salad plates. Place a warm, baked filo packet on top, and crown with the warm preserve dressing. A good grinding of pepper makes a perfect finish.

- 3 sheets of filo pastry (about 13 × 18 inches / 33 × 45 cm)
- Oil for brushing
- 8 oz (250 g) brie or Camembert cheese
- 1 Tbsp (15 mL) olive oil
- 1 small shallot, diced
- ⅔ cup (160 mL) cherry preserves (I use Brickstone's cherry and calvados)
- 1 Tbsp (15 mL) brandy
- 6 cups (1.5 L) baby spinach leaves (or salad mix)
- Good-quality olive oil for drizzling
- Sea salt
- Freshly ground pepper

IN A PINCH

Go ahead: use prewashed baby spinach. Just check the bag or container carefully to make sure the leaves look fresh.

Filo-Wrapped Greens
with Mustard Balsamic Dressing

When you are searching for that wow factor for a lunch or dinner party, look no further! The simple technique of forming filo pastry into a ring not only looks fantastic, it provides a great crunch to an otherwise pedestrian salad. See page 122 for more ways to use filo. This recipe is pictured on the cover.

Serves 6

To prepare the filo bands, lay one sheet of filo on your work surface, brush lightly with olive oil, and sprinkle with about 1 heaping Tbsp (15 mL+) of Parmesan. Cut sheet in half lengthwise. Take each half and fold it lengthwise two times to create a band about 1½ inches (4 cm) wide. Repeat with remaining filo sheets.

Lightly oil a six-cup muffin pan and fit a band of filo inside each cup, lightly pressing it against the sides of the cup to create a cavity. Take the six sheets of foil and scrunch them up to golf-ball size. Place the foil balls inside the cups.

Bake in a preheated 350°F (180°C) oven for 5 to 8 minutes until the filo is golden and crispy. Remove from the oven, take out the foil balls, and let cool.

While the filo cools, place the greens in a big bowl and set aside.

For the dressing, whisk together the vinegar, mustard, and garlic in a bowl. Slowly pour in the oil, whisking the entire time. The dressing will thicken as you whisk. Season with sea salt and pepper. Toss the dressing over the greens.

To serve, place one filo band on each plate. Fill the opening with the dressed greens; stick in the avocado slices and some of the sprouts (if using), so that they stand upright. Arrange the tomatoes along the edge of your salad plate and scatter the remaining sprouts along the edges as well. Sprinkle pine nuts on top.

Squeeze the balsamic glaze artistically over the plate and serve immediately.

Filo-Wrapped Greens

- 3 sheets of filo pastry (about 13 × 18 inches / 33 × 45 cm)
- Olive oil for brushing
- ¼ cup (60 mL) grated Parmesan cheese
- Six 4- × 6-inch (10 × 15 cm) sheets of foil
- 3 heaping cups (750 mL+) mixed greens
- 2 ripe avocados, peeled and thinly sliced
- 1 cup (250 mL) mustard or sunflower sprouts (optional)
- 1 cup (250 mL) grape (or cherry) tomatoes, halved
- ½ cup (125 mL) toasted pine nuts
- Balsamic Glaze (page 157) for finishing

Mustard Balsamic Dressing

- 2 Tbsp (30 mL) aged balsamic vinegar
- 2 Tbsp (30 mL) Dijon mustard
- 1 clove garlic, minced
- ½ cup (125 mL) extra virgin olive oil
- Sea salt
- Freshly ground pepper

Santa Fe Rice Salad
with Ancho Chili Dressing

The interesting texture in this salad comes from jicama, a crunchy, moist vegetable that is like a cross between an apple and daikon radish. It gives interest and contrast to what would otherwise be a plain old rice salad.

Serves 6 to 8

Make the dressing first. Soften the dried peppers in the hot water for at least 1 hour.

When rehydrated, remove from the water, cut off the stems, remove seeds, and finely chop. Transfer to a bowl, along with the vinegar, shallots, garlic, cilantro, and lime-infused olive oil. Whisk to combine. Season with sea salt and pepper to taste.

Combine all the salad ingredients in a large bowl. Pour dressing overtop and toss to mix well.

IN A PINCH

Jicama has a thin papery brown skin that needs to be peeled. Once you have peeled the jicama, put it directly into acidulated water to prevent browning.

Leftovers are great for an impromptu lunch or a side dish for dinner. This salad uses leftover rice, whether it's jasmine, basmati, or just plain Texas white. Easy, easy—and the rich dressing adds that gourmet touch. And canned black beans are just fine.

Ancho Chili Dressing

- 4 dried ancho chilies
- 1 cup (250 mL) hot water
- ¼ cup (60 mL) rice vinegar
- 2 large shallots, diced
- 2 cloves garlic, minced
- ⅓ cup (80 mL) chopped fresh cilantro
- ⅔ cup (160 mL) lime-infused olive oil (page 67)
- Sea salt
- Freshly ground pepper

Rice Salad

- 3 cups (750 mL) cooked rice
- 2 cups (500 mL) cooked black turtle beans
- 1 heaping cup (250 mL+) diced jicama (peeled)
- 1 red pepper, cored and diced
- 1 large mango, peeled and diced

Spinach Salad with Pears and Glazed Pecans

Here's another great spinach salad you can put together in minutes (especially if you buy prewashed spinach). It's amazing how one simple condiment like balsamic glaze can heighten simple foods like pears and add a sweet crunch to nuts. Spinach salad never tasted so good. Balsamic glaze is available in all good gourmet stores, and I also provide a recipe on page 157.

The first time I made this salad, I made the mistake of setting the glazed pecans on the table. My guests polished them off in less than five minutes. So a word of advice—either hide your garnish, or triple the amount of glazed nuts and serve them with wine. They make a great cocktail nibble.

Serves 4

For the glazed pecans, toss the nuts with the balsamic glaze and place on a parchment-lined tray. Bake in a preheated 275°F (140°C) oven for about 15 minutes. Remove and let cool. Set aside for garnish.

For the dressing, place the vinegar and mustard in a bowl; stir to combine. Slowly whisk in the oil until the dressing becomes thick and smooth. Season with sea salt and pepper to taste.

Place the butter in a nonstick pan, add the pears, and toss to coat; add the glaze and continue to sauté for about 4 minutes. Turn off the heat.

To serve the salad, pour the dressing over the spinach; toss well to coat. Divide evenly among four side plates or bowls. Lay the sautéed pear slices overtop; garnish with the toasted nuts and small dollops of chèvre. Finish with freshly ground pepper.

Glazed Pecans
- 1 cup (250 mL) pecans (or almonds, walnuts, or hazelnuts)
- 3 Tbsp (45 mL) Balsamic Glaze (page 157)

Pear Vinaigrette
- 3 Tbsp (45 mL) pear vinegar
- 2 tsp (10 mL) Dijon mustard
- ⅔ cup (160 mL) good-quality olive oil
- Sea salt
- Freshly ground pepper

Salad
- 2 Tbsp (30 mL) unsalted butter
- 2 firm pears (Bosc or Anjou), cored and sliced in eighths
- 3 Tbsp (45 mL) Balsamic Glaze (page 157)
- 6 heaping handfuls of baby spinach
- ½ cup (125 mL) soft chèvre (garnish)
- Freshly ground pepper

IN A PINCH

Pear vinegar has an unmistakable taste that brings life to spinach. It's a must-have for your pantry.

Mixed Green Salad
with Raspberry Chipotle Vinaigrette

Imagine—a delicious dressing made from three ingredients. You can take simple greens to a new level just by combining a good olive oil and balsamic vinegar with raspberry chipotle sauce. Voilà! Truly a sensational twist on oil and vinegar.

Serves 6

Whisk the vinegar and the raspberry chipotle sauce together in a bowl. Slowly whisk in the oil until the dressing emulsifies.

To serve, divide greens among six plates or bowls. Drizzle vinaigrette overtop, arrange avocado, carrot, and tomatoes on the greens, and finish with a pinch of fleur de sel and freshly ground pepper. The remainder of the vinaigrette will keep up to three weeks, chilled.

IN A PINCH

Raspberry chipotle sauce is a condiment that also doubles as a marinade. There are several brands on the market. It makes a great vinaigrette and is a yummy topper for baked brie or a glaze for chicken breasts.

Raspberry Chipotle Vinaigrette
- ¼ cup (60 mL) balsamic vinegar (I use an 8-year-old balsamic)
- ⅓ cup (80 mL) raspberry chipotle sauce
- ⅔ cup (160 mL) extra virgin olive oil

Salad
- 6 cups (1.5 L) mixed greens
- 1 ripe avocado, peeled and sliced
- 1 carrot, julienned
- 1 cup (250 mL) halved grape tomatoes or quartered large tomatoes
- Fleur de sel
- Freshly ground pepper

Tabbouleh Salad

The bulgur and cucumber make this a light and delicious salad that marries well with chicken, lamb, or fish. The welcome addition of fresh herbs brightens the flavor profile.

Serves 6 to 8

Place the bulgur in a large bowl; pour the boiling water over and cover. Let it sit for an hour.

While bulgur is soaking, make the dressing by combining lemon juice, garlic, and preserved lemon. Slowly whisk in the oil until the dressing emulsifies, and season with salt and pepper to taste.

When the bulgur is ready, toss with the dressing to coat evenly. Add the cucumber, tomatoes, fresh herbs, and green onions. Stir to combine and serve immediately.

- 1 cup (250 mL) bulgur wheat
- 1½ cups (375 mL) boiling water
- 2 cups (500 mL) diced Japanese cucumber
- 2 cups (500 mL) grape tomatoes, halved
- 1 bunch Italian parsley, finely chopped
- 1 cup (250 mL) minced fresh cilantro
- ½ cup (125 mL) finely chopped fresh mint
- 4 green onions, thinly sliced

Lemon Dressing
- Juice of ½ lemon
- 1 clove garlic, minced
- 1 Tbsp (15 mL) chopped preserved lemon
- ⅔ cup (160 mL) extra virgin olive oil
- Sea salt
- Freshly ground pepper

7-Grain Salad with Orange Dressing

I would describe this salad as nutritious and interesting. Crunch and texture are my favorite elements in food. This salad can be served hot or cold, alongside a main course or as lunch. The simple orange dressing is delicious, but feel free to experiment. Try sun-dried fruits, like cranberries, blueberries, or apricots. Pecans make a nice nut substitute.

Serves 6

Bring the water (or stock) to the boil; add the rice mix and butter. Bring back to a boil; reduce heat, cover tightly, and simmer for 35 to 40 minutes.

In the meantime, combine all the orange dressing ingredients together. Taste and adjust seasoning and set aside.

When the rice is cooked, remove from heat, and place in a serving bowl. Pour the dressing over; add the figs and stir to combine. If you are serving the rice hot, add the herbs, top with toasted pumpkin seeds, and serve immediately. If you are serving the rice at room temperature, let it cool, and just before serving, add the herbs and top with the pumpkin seeds.

IN A PINCH

Mixing several kinds of rice and grains yourself could be fun, but rice mixes can easily be purchased in most grocery stores. There are so many different blends and mixes available, and when you're in a pinch, it's just one quick trip to the store and you can whip up this salad in no time at all.

7-Grain Salad

- 2½ cups (625 mL) water (or vegetable or chicken stock)
- 1 cup (250 mL) 7-grain rice mix
- 1 tsp (5 mL) unsalted butter
- ¾ cup (185 mL) dried Black Mission figs, cut into quarters
- ½ cup (125 mL) chopped fresh mint
- ½ cup (125 mL) chopped Italian parsley
- ½ cup (125 mL) toasted pumpkin seeds

Orange Dressing

- Zest of 1 orange
- ⅓ cup (80 mL) freshly squeezed orange juice
- 1 medium shallot, finely diced
- 1 small clove garlic, minced
- ½ cup (125 mL) extra virgin olive oil
- Sea salt
- Freshly ground pepper

Mediterranean Orzo Salad

Pasta salads come and go without much fanfare. This orzo salad is by far the tastiest one I've created in a long time. Orzo is the rice-shaped pasta that cooks up tender but light—unlike "heavy" pastas, the orzo allows the flavors of the dressing to shine.

Serves 6 to 8

Cook the orzo in plenty of boiling salted water. Do not overcook—just cook until it's al dente. Drain and give the pasta one quick rinse of cold water. Transfer to a serving bowl and pour the ½ cup (125 mL) of lemon-infused olive oil over, tossing to coat. This will prevent the pasta from sticking together.

Heat the 3 Tbsp (45 mL) of olive oil in a frying pan; add the onions and fry for 5 minutes until they just begin to brown. Pour in the balsamic vinegar and let simmer for 5 more minutes.

Remove the onions from the pan with a spoon and add to the orzo. Add the artichokes and chopped garlic to the same frying pan. Pan-fry for 3 to 5 minutes, seasoning with sea salt and a bit of pepper.

Add this to the orzo mixture along with the olives and herbs. Stir well to combine. Garnish with the crumbled cheese and serve.

IN A PINCH

O Olive Oil, from California, makes wonderful organic citrus-infused olive oils. If lemon- or lime-infused olive oil is not available, add 1 tsp (5 mL) lemon/lime zest to 1 cup (250 mL) extra virgin olive oil. You can use it here, and in other dressings and marinades.

- 2 cups (500 mL) orzo pasta
- ½ cup (125 mL) lemon-infused olive oil
- 3 Tbsp (45 mL) olive oil
- 15 fresh or frozen silverskin onions or pearl onions, peeled if fresh
- ½ cup (125 mL) balsamic vinegar
- One 14 oz (398 mL) can artichokes, drained and cut into sixths
- 3 cloves garlic, chopped
- 1 tsp (5 mL) sea salt
- Freshly ground Tellicherry (or black) pepper
- ⅔ cup (160 mL) chopped kalamata olives
- ⅓ cup (80 mL) chopped fresh mint
- ⅓ cup (80 mL) chopped fresh cilantro
- 8 oz (250 g) feta cheese, crumbled (garnish)

Hearts of Palm and Sweet Onion Salad with Mango and Poppy Seed Dressing

Hearts of palm are the "lost" canned vegetable that really deserves a place in your kitchen. The cool crunch and pearl white color work well in this bright-tasting salad.

Serves 6

Drain the hearts of palm and wrap in paper towel to soak up excess moisture. Julienne the hearts the size of matchsticks and place in a glass salad bowl. Slice the onion as thinly as possible, cut the blanched asparagus in half lengthwise, julienne the peppers, and add all of these to the bowl. Cover with plastic wrap and chill until serving.

Whisk the mango vinaigrette, mustard, and ginger together in a medium bowl. Slowly pour in the olive oil, whisking the entire time to emulsify. The dressing will thicken as you whisk. Add the poppy seeds, sea salt, and ground pepper.

To serve, pour half the dressing over the chilled vegetables and toss gently to coat. Add more dressing to suit your tastes.

IN A PINCH

If you can't find mango vinaigrette, mash half of a fresh mango into pulp using a small food processor, potato masher, or fork. Stir in 2 Tbsp (30 mL) of fresh lemon juice.

Prepare the undressed salad a few hours ahead of time and keep chilled until you are ready to serve. You can also make the dressing a few days in advance and keep it chilled.

Salad
- One 14 oz (398 mL) can hearts of palm
- 1 sweet onion
- ½ lb (250 g) asparagus, blanched and cooled
- 1 red pepper, cored
- 1 yellow pepper, cored

Mango Poppy Seed Dressing
- ⅓ cup (80 mL) mango vinaigrette (store-bought)
- 2 Tbsp (30 mL) Dijon mustard
- 1 Tbsp (15 mL) freshly minced ginger
- ⅔ cup (160 mL) extra virgin olive oil
- 1 Tbsp (15 mL) poppy seeds
- Sea salt
- Freshly ground pepper

Roasted Corn Salad

Whenever I see fresh corn on the cob being sold, I immediately snap it up and rush home to grill it to perfection. I featured this recipe on *The Bill Good Show* one year. It was late August, just as fresh corn was becoming available in local markets. Ian Koningsfest, the program director at CKNW, suggested a good crumble of goat or feta cheese would add just that little bit more. He was right!

Serves 6 to 8

To make the dressing, whisk together the garlic, mustard, and champagne vinegar. Slowly whisk in the lemon olive oil to emulsify it. The dressing will thicken as you whisk. Season with sea salt and pepper. Set aside.

Heat the barbecue to medium-high. Husk corn and remove silk. When the barbecue is hot, grill the cobs until they are darkened on all sides. Cool and cut the kernels from the cobs. You should have about 4 cups (1 L) of corn. Set aside.

Grill the pepper and the onion pieces until lightly browned on both sides. I like to brush them with a bit of olive oil while they are grilling. Remove, cool, and chop into small dice the size of the corn kernels (there is no need to skin the pepper). Add to the bowl of corn and mix in both the edamame and black beans and chopped jalapeño. Season to taste with salt and pepper.

Pour the dressing over the corn salad and toss to mix evenly. Garnish with cilantro and crumbled cheese (if using).

IN A PINCH

To easily remove the corn kernels from the cob, stand the cob on one end in a large shallow serving bowl or on a dinner plate. Cut with a serrated knife; the kernels will fall into the bowl without a mess. If you are a kitchen tool junkie, there are very cool tools that will do the job for you with ease.

Champagne Lemon Dressing

- 1 large clove garlic, minced
- 1 heaping Tbsp (15 mL+) Dijon mustard
- ¼ cup (60 mL) champagne vinegar
- ⅔ cup (160 mL) lemon-infused olive oil (page 67)
- Sea salt
- Freshly ground pepper

Roasted Corn Salad

- 4 cobs fresh corn
- 1 large red pepper, cored and cut into quarters
- 1 large sweet onion, cut into quarters, root end intact
- 1½ cups (375 mL) edamame beans, cooked and shelled
- One 12 oz (355 mL) can black beans, drained and rinsed
- 2 Tbsp (30 mL) finely chopped pickled jalapeño peppers
- Sea salt
- Freshly ground pepper

Options for Garnish

- ½ cup (125 mL) chopped fresh cilantro
- ½ cup (125 mL) crumbled feta or chèvre

Panzanella
(Tuscan Bread Salad)

The juicy ripeness of tomatoes along with the fruity nuances of the olive oil provide the moisture for the day-old bread in this salad. So simple and so good! "Cracked green olives" are usually marinated in herbs and lemon, but you can use any olive of your choice.

Serves 6

Place the cubed bread in a large bowl. Cut the tomatoes into large dice and add them to the bread along with any juice that the tomatoes may release.

Whisk together all the dressing ingredients. Pour over the bread and tomatoes. Pit the olives. Add the olives, along with the onion, basil, parsley leaves, and capers.

Toss the salad together; season to taste with fleur de sel and pepper and serve. The longer the salad sits, the softer the bread becomes and the more flavorful the salad.

IN A PINCH

This is the perfect salad in which to use any leftover expensive artisan loaves. Trust the Italians to create a salad with such a purpose. If you have leftover bread, store in a freezer baggie and freeze until you want to make this salad.

- ▸ 3 heaping cups (750 mL+) cubed day-old rustic bread
- ▸ 5 very ripe Roma (or any heirloom) tomatoes
- ▸ ½ cup (125 mL) cracked green, Picholine, or kalamata olives
- ▸ 1 cup (250 mL) thinly sliced sweet onion
- ▸ ½ cup (125 mL) torn fresh basil leaves
- ▸ ¼ cup (60 mL) Italian parsley leaves
- ▸ 1 Tbsp (15 mL) capers, drained
- ▸ Fleur de sel
- ▸ Freshly ground Tellicherry (or black) pepper

Dressing
- ▸ ¼ cup (60 mL) balsamic vinegar
- ▸ 1 large clove garlic, minced
- ▸ ⅔ cup (160 mL) extra virgin olive oil

Warm Wild Salmon Salad

When fresh B.C. salmon run, so should you—to your local fish market to get your share. Nothing can compare to the incredible taste of wild salmon grilled to perfection. I like to cook a bit more than I need for dinner so as to have some on hand for lunch the next day.

Serves 6

Preheat barbecue to medium-high heat.

Slather the flesh side of the salmon with the barbecue sauce. Place the salmon skin side down on the barbecue. Brush the asparagus with a little olive oil and add to the barbecue. Do not turn the salmon; cook it through on one side only, being careful not to overcook it (make sure it stays moist). Check on the asparagus, as it will be done faster.

While the salmon and asparagus cook, heat the butter in a frying pan; add the sliced mushrooms, and sauté on high heat to brown. Season with a pinch of sea salt and freshly ground pepper to taste.

Place the salad greens and tomatoes in a large bowl, drizzle with the olive oil and balsamic vinegar, season with salt and pepper to taste, and toss.

To serve, heap the greens onto oversized serving plates or bowls. Add a portion of mushrooms, a few spears of asparagus, and a piece of the salmon in the center. Garnish with the olives and a good sprinkling of feta (if using).

IN A PINCH

To prevent mushrooms from releasing moisture, sauté them on high heat and just a bit of butter or oil. Do not add any liquid and watch how quickly they brown.

Break free and use your favorite prewashed mixed greens and your favorite bottled barbecue sauce. I like to support our own local chef Ann Kirsebom, who has created a line of great marinades and sauces. Tequi-Lime barbecue sauce is my favorite.

Salmon

- 2½ lb (1.25 kg) whole fillet of wild B.C. salmon
- 1 cup (250 mL) your favorite barbecue sauce
- 1 lb (500 g) asparagus
- Drizzle of olive oil
- 2 Tbsp (30 mL) unsalted butter
- 2 cups (500 mL) your choice of mixed mushrooms
- Pinch of sea salt
- Freshly ground pepper

Salad

- 3 cups (750 mL) assorted salad greens, washed
- 3 large yellow (or red) tomatoes, cut into quarters (or equivalent amount of cherry tomatoes, halved)
- ⅔ cup (160 mL) extra virgin olive oil
- ¼ cup (60 mL) balsamic vinegar
- Pinch of sea salt
- Freshly ground pepper

Options for Garnish

- 1 cup (250 mL) oil-cured olives
- 1 cup (250 mL) crumbled feta cheese

Spanish Tuna Salad with Crispy Shallots

Smoked Spanish paprika, as a rub, enhances tuna with a deep, smoky flavor. The crispy shallots make for a really different main course salad. I prefer the peppery taste of arugula to the mixed greens, but both work well.

Serves 6

Start by making the crispy shallots. Dredge the sliced shallots in flour and shake off the excess. Heat 2 Tbsp (30 mL) of olive oil in a nonstick frying pan; add the flour-coated shallots and fry on medium heat, stirring constantly to promote even browning. A note of caution: they start slow and then brown relatively fast, so stay on top of the stirring. Remove from the pan with a slotted spoon and blot on paper towels.

Whisk dressing ingredients together in a small bowl.

Toss olives, capers, piquillo peppers, and pine nuts together in another bowl.

Rub the paprika onto both sides of the tuna. Heat olive oil in a large frying pan over medium-high heat; sear the tuna 2 to 3 minutes per side for rare, 4 to 5 minutes for medium. Remove tuna from the pan and set aside.

To serve, place the grilled tuna on a bed of arugula (or mixed greens). Top each piece of tuna with the olive and caper mixture, and drizzle with the dressing. Garnish with the crispy shallots.

IN A PINCH

If you can't find piquillo peppers, use jarred roasted red peppers. Make sure to drain and pat with a paper towel to dry.

Crispy shallots are also sold in cans and are available from good gourmet stores.

Crispy Shallots

- 4 large shallots, thinly sliced
- Unbleached all-purpose flour for dredging
- 2 Tbsp (30 mL) olive oil for frying shallots

Dressing

- ¾ cup (185 mL) extra virgin olive oil
- ¼ cup (60 mL) sherry vinegar
- 1 large clove garlic, minced
- 1 tsp (5 mL) lemon zest
- Sea salt
- Freshly ground Tellicherry (or black) pepper

Tuna Salad

- 1 cup (250 mL) oil-cured olives
- 3 Tbsp (45 mL) capers, drained
- One 7 oz (200 g) jar piquillo peppers, drained and sliced
- ¾ cup (185 mL) toasted pine nuts
- 3 Tbsp (45 mL) smoked Spanish paprika
- 6 yellowfin or Ahi tuna steaks (about 5 oz/150 g each, or whatever size you prefer)
- 2 Tbsp (30 mL) olive oil for searing tuna
- 6 cups (1.5 L) arugula (or mixed greens)

Chili Chicken Cashew Salad
with Ginger Mango Dressing

This salad is a terrific main course for dinner or a complex lunch entrée. Poaching the chicken in a coconut milk broth brings a mellow sweetness to this salad, and the store-bought condiments used in the dressing introduce savory, sweet, and spicy dimensions. All of the ingredients here are easy to find in local supermarkets and gourmet stores. The buckwheat noodles can be interchanged with either jasmine rice or cellophane noodles. If mango is not available, substitute papaya.

Serves 6 to 8

Chicken
- 2 whole boneless, skinless chicken breasts, preferably free-range
- One 14 oz (398 mL) can coconut milk
- 1 cup (250 mL) chicken stock
- 3 Tbsp (45 mL) rice vinegar
- 2 Tbsp (30 mL) fish sauce
- 1 stalk lemongrass (white part only), finely chopped
- 1 Tbsp (15 mL) finely grated fresh ginger

Halve each chicken breast lengthwise and pound to an even thickness.

Mix the remaining ingredients for the chicken together in a large frying pan. Bring the mixture to a slow simmer; add the breasts in a single layer and poach for 5 minutes. Turn and poach for 5 minutes on the other side until they are cooked through but not overdone. Discard the liquid; remove the breasts, and set aside to cool.

Continued on following page.

Continued

Ginger Mango Dressing

- 3 Tbsp (45 mL) mango chutney
- 2 Tbsp (30 mL) sweet chili sauce
- 2 Tbsp (30 mL) fresh lime juice
- 2 Tbsp (30 mL) fish sauce
- 2 Tbsp (30 mL) rice vinegar
- 1 Tbsp (15 mL) light muscovado (or brown) sugar
- 2 Tbsp (30 mL) freshly minced ginger
- 1 clove garlic, minced
- 1 tsp (5 mL) lime zest
- 1 cup (250 mL) grapeseed oil
- Sea salt
- Freshly ground pepper

For the ginger mango dressing, combine all the ingredients except the oil. Slowly whisk in the oil to emulsify it. Taste the dressing and adjust seasoning with sea salt and pepper.

Salad

- 3 cups (750 mL) cooked buckwheat noodles
- 2 cups (500 mL) thinly sliced celery
- 25 blanched snap peas
- ½ English cucumber, sliced
- 1 cup (250 mL) torn fresh mint leaves
- 1 cup (250 mL) torn fresh cilantro leaves
- 1 cup (250 mL) torn fresh basil leaves
- 1 stalk lemongrass (white part only), finely chopped
- 1 small mango (or papaya), peeled and thickly diced
- 1 cup (250 mL) chopped cashews (garnish)
- 3 Tbsp (45 mL) black sesame seeds (optional garnish)

To assemble the salad, lay the noodles on the base of your serving platter. Lightly toss together the celery, snap peas, cucumber, fresh herbs, and lemongrass. Toss this mixture with half the dressing and spread over the noodles. To serve, slice the cooked chicken into julienne and lay it over the veggies. Sprinkle the cubes of mango (or papaya) overtop and garnish with chopped cashews and black sesame seeds (if using). Drizzle the remaining dressing overtop and serve.

10 Must-Have Ingredients

1   **Amaretti cookies**
I make a lot of fruit-based desserts, and instead of using soda crackers or tapioca to absorb the juices, I always crumble two or three cookies over the fruit. As the fruit releases juices, the cookie crumbs absorb them. Try amaretti cookies in a crumble or mixed with melted chocolate, which hardens into an interesting little chocolate haystack (a nice alternative to coconut).

2   **Risotto**
We eat risotto in our house at least once a week. I have at least four pounds of this rice on hand at any given time. Carnaroli or Vialone Nano are good choices, especially if they are "superfino" (refers to the grain size). Stir on!

3   **Capers**
Capers add zing to pasta sauces and fish. Deep-frying them in vegetable oil for about 45 seconds gives you an amazing garnish: the caper opens into a little flower and has a bit of a crunch. Make sure you dry them well before plunging them into the oil!

4   **Chicken stock base**
I prefer the concentrated paste variety (try the Major brand). You adjust the intensity of the stock by deciding how much to dilute it. You can also add 1 tsp (5 mL) of undiluted paste to perk up a dull sauce.

5   **Dijon mustard**
This mustard is an essential component of salad dressings, marinades, aioli, and don't forget the good ol' ham sandwich!

6   **Fleur de sel**
I love this wonderful, perfectly structured sea salt from France. An absolute *must*. (But not for cooking; just for finishing.)

7   Jarred lemon curd

This is my miracle dessert helper in a jar! You can combine the curd with an equal portion of whipped cream and use as a pie filling, or make the supersimple Lemon Tart on page 194. Or you can just spoon the curd directly into little store-bought prebaked tart shells and top each with a fresh berry.

8   Moroccan spice rub

I always have several flavors of rubs on hand, but the Moroccan is far and away my favorite. It has just the right balance of heat and spice. I use it on fish, chicken, lamb, and sweet potatoes (see pages 121 and 144). NoMU and Cote d'Azur are two really good brands.

9   Olive oil

You need regular olive oil for cooking, and a fancier olive oil for finishing dishes and for salads—make sure you have at least two kinds of fancy olive oil. Flavors are diverse, so experiment to find your favorites.

10   Panko

To me, this is the undisputed king of crumbs. These Japanese breadcrumbs produce a crisp, dry coating that never gets soggy. I use it to bread fish, chicken, and even vegetables. Every kitchen must have a least one bag in the cupboard. Two is better!

Main Courses

Pancetta and Veggie Pasta

We enjoy pasta in our house at least twice a week. The ingredients are seldom the same and always dependent on what is in the fridge. This recipe is a recent favorite. It's full of flavor and easy to prepare for two guests or 20. Capers always add the *za za zoom* to any dish.

Serves 4

Cook pasta in boiling salted water until al dente.

While the pasta is cooking, heat the oil in a large saucepan; add the onion and pancetta and sauté until golden. Stir in the capers and mushrooms. Toss and continue to sauté for another 3 minutes.

Add the chopped asparagus and tomatoes, and toss again. Add the chili flakes or paste (if using), basil, and cream. Let the sauce simmer for 5 minutes or so. When the pasta is almost done, spoon off a ladleful of the foamy pasta water and add it to the sauce. Season with sea salt and pepper to taste.

Drain the pasta and add it to the sauce. Toss well to coat and serve immediately with lots of shavings of fresh Parmesan.

- ½ lb (250 g) your favorite dry pasta
- 2 Tbsp (30 mL) olive oil
- ½ cup (125 mL) diced onion
- ½ cup (125 mL) diced pancetta
- 1 Tbsp (15 mL) capers, drained
- 5 large button mushrooms, sliced
- 5 spears asparagus, chopped
- 4 Roma tomatoes, diced
- 1 tsp (5 mL) chili flakes or paste (optional)
- ⅓ cup (80 mL) chopped fresh basil
- ⅓ cup (80 mL) whipping cream
- Sea salt
- Freshly ground pepper
- Shaved Parmesan cheese (garnish)

Cheese Fondue

The most popular fondues are chocolate and cheese for the simple reason that they are just that—simple. Classic cheese fondue combines the best of Swiss cheeses: Gruyère and Emmenthal. With these two classics, you are free to add whatever your taste buds crave. Add fontina for a creamier fondue or Appenzeller for that hint of piquant. Or both! Cube a selection of breads (not just boring white)—try green olive, rosemary, or fig. All and any would enhance your fondue experience. Enjoy!

Serves 4 to 6

To roast garlic, cut ¼ inch (6 mm) off the top of the garlic head; rub with oil, wrap loosely in foil, and bake for 1 hour in a preheated 325°F (160°C) oven until the garlic is soft and golden brown. Cool and remove papery skin. Set aside.

Place the wine and kirsch in the fondue pot and bring to a simmer. Shake the grated cheeses together with the flour in a medium to large Ziploc bag; the idea here is to dredge the cheese with the flour.

Add the cheese, a heaping handful at a time, to the simmering wine, stirring well and waiting for each handful to be melted before adding the next one.

Continue to add and stir until you have used all the cheese. Season with pepper and a pinch of nutmeg.

Serve with plenty of assorted breads and blanched vegetables for dipping. Cubes of poached chicken are also a nice addition.

- ▸ 1 whole head garlic
- ▸ Olive oil for roasting garlic
- ▸ 1 cup (250 mL) Chablis or Riesling wine
- ▸ 1 Tbsp (15 mL) kirsch liqueur
- ▸ 1 cup (250 mL) grated Gruyère
- ▸ 1 cup (250 mL) grated Emmenthal
- ▸ 1 cup (250 mL) grated fontina
- ▸ ½ cup (125 mL) grated Appenzeller cheese
- ▸ 1 Tbsp (15 mL) unbleached all-purpose flour
- ▸ Good grinding of Tellicherry (or black) pepper
- ▸ Pinch of grated nutmeg

IN A PINCH

When you know you're going to be short on time the day of the fondue party, cube the bread and blanch or steam the vegetables the day before. Some ideas for vegetables: mini potatoes, broccoli, cauliflower, button mushrooms (raw or cooked and kept whole), snow peas. Go wild!

Thai Prawns

My dear friend Bob Lawrence is a British expat. He married my best friend, Diane, but (unbeknownst to him at the time) he married me as well. He had no cooking skills way back then, but he was a hell of a handyman. I call him Bob the Builder, but he'd prefer the Canadian version of Jamie Oliver. Bob does make the best Thai food I have ever eaten outside Bangkok. When he exchanges his hammer for the whisk, we all line up. I hope you enjoy his creation as much as we do.

Serves 4 to 6

Heat the oil on medium-high in a large frying pan. Add the mustard seeds, chilies, curry and lime leaves, and garlic and cook for 1 minute.

Add the shallots and ginger and sauté for another minute, taking care not to burn the shallots. Then add the coconut milk, water, and turmeric and simmer for 10 minutes.

Add the prawns and simmer slowly for about 5 minutes until they are bright pink.

Serve as an appie with naan triangles or as a main course with basmati rice.

- ¼ cup (60 mL) grapeseed oil
- 1 tsp (5 mL) mustard seeds
- 3 red or green Thai chilies, finely chopped
- 10 fresh curry leaves
- 5 kaffir lime leaves
- 2 cloves garlic, minced
- 4 small shallots, finely chopped
- 2 Tbsp (30 mL) finely chopped fresh ginger
- One 14 oz (398 mL) can coconut milk
- ¼ cup (60 mL) water
- 2 tsp (10 mL) ground turmeric
- 30 fresh prawns (26/30 count), peeled and deveined

Brined and Grilled Prawns

Brining isn't just for turkeys; it works wonders on prawns too.

Serves 4 to 6

Place the salt in a large bowl; add the boiling water, stir to dissolve the salt, and then stir in the cold water. Add the prawns to the brine (you can add them frozen). Let them soak for 45 minutes.

In the meantime, mix the paste ingredients in a small bowl. When prawns are ready, drain, rinse, and blot them dry. Rub with the paste.

Grill on the barbecue or pan-fry on high heat for 5 minutes until prawns turn bright pink. To serve, garnish with the finely chopped cilantro.

IN A PINCH

Harissa is a spicy chili paste that hails from Morocco. You can use any chili paste if harissa is not available.

As mentioned, the prawns can be added to the brine frozen—a great shortcut when you've forgotten to defrost them!

Prawns

- ▸ 1 cup (250 mL) kosher salt
- ▸ 1 cup (250 mL) boiling water
- ▸ 8 cups (2 L) cold water
- ▸ 1 lb (500 g) fresh prawns (26/30 count), shells kept on

Paste

- ▸ 2 cloves garlic, minced
- ▸ 2 Tbsp (30 mL) sweet smoked Spanish paprika
- ▸ 1 Tbsp (15 mL) harissa
- ▸ 3 Tbsp (45 mL) olive oil
- ▸ Juice of ½ lemon
- ▸ Sea salt
- ▸ Freshly ground pepper

- ▸ ½ cup (125 mL) minced fresh cilantro (garnish)

Monkfish en Papillote

Monkfish is commonly referred to as poor man's lobster. The texture is similar, but the taste is much lighter. Papillote is a method of cooking that has somehow faded from the culinary scene of late. It involves making an envelope out of parchment paper and baking the fish in the package. The benefits are many: the steam within the package keeps the fish moist, and the presentation on the plate is interesting to say the least.

Serves 6

Heat the butter in a large frying pan; add the shallots, garlic, carrots, and celery and sauté for about 5 minutes. Add the mushrooms, parsley, and salt and pepper to taste. Cook for another 3 minutes, being careful not to overcook the veggies. Cool.

Fold a piece of the parchment in half and butter one half well all the way to the edge. Place a portion of the cooled sautéed veggies on the buttered half, top with a piece of the fish, and sprinkle with a drizzle of white wine (or vermouth). Fold the top half over the bottom half and crimp the edges to seal. Repeat with the remaining parchment.

Bake in a preheated 400°F (200°C) oven for 5 minutes; reduce the heat to 350°F (180°C) and bake for another 10 to 12 minutes.

To serve, place each parchment package on a dinner plate, bring to the table, and cut the packages open, releasing the fragrant aromas.

- ¼ cup (60 mL) unsalted butter
- 3 shallots, diced
- 2 cloves garlic, minced
- 2 large carrots, peeled and julienned
- 2 stalks celery, julienned
- 1 cup (250 mL) sliced fresh shiitake mushrooms
- ¼ cup (60 mL) finely chopped parsley
- Sea salt
- Freshly ground Tellicherry (or black) pepper

- Parchment paper cut into six 8-inch (20 cm) circles or hearts (hearts may work better depending on the shape of your fish)
- 2 lb (1 kg) fresh monkfish (or halibut, cod, or sablefish), in 6 pieces
- White wine (or vermouth) for sprinkling

Salmon Burgers

If you live in British Columbia, salmon is *the* fish of choice. We all serve salmon frequently and offer it to out-of-town guests at every opportunity. Salmon, you could say, is our "show-off" fish. These burgers are a nice change from the overserved steaks or fillets—our show-off fish still shines. The Mediterranean Orzo Salad (page 67) makes a great side dish.

Serves 4

Mince the salmon into a size that resembles ground hamburger by rocking a chef's knife back and forth against the fish on the cutting board. Mix with the remaining patty ingredients in a medium bowl until well combined.

Form into four patties and pan-fry on medium-high heat or grill on a barbecue for 5 minutes on each side. To serve, split the buns open, and garnish patties with your favorite burger toppings.

IN A PINCH

Most good fishmongers will have premade salmon burgers. They're not as good as these, but they'll do in a pinch.

Great salmon burger toppings:
- Chili aioli
- Pesto sauce
- Chutney
- Baby spinach leaves
- Thinly sliced sweet onion
- Avocado
- Sautéed mushrooms
- Crisp bacon or pancetta
- Anything your imagination comes up with...

- 1 lb (500 g) fresh coho, sockeye, or spring salmon, skin removed
- 2 cloves garlic, minced
- 2 large shallots, thinly sliced
- 2 Tbsp (30 mL) grapeseed oil
- 1 Tbsp (15 mL) capers, drained and chopped
- 1 tsp (5 mL) lemon zest
- 1 Tbsp (15 mL) unbleached all-purpose flour
- 1 large egg
- Heaping ¼ cup (60 mL+) chopped fresh dill
- Sea salt
- Fresh coarsely ground pepper

- 4 crusty buns

Pan-Seared Halibut with Vegetables

Most of this recipe can be preprepped in order to save loads of stress. At serving time, simply reheat the preroasted vegetables while the halibut is finishing in the oven. Both salmon and sablefish are good substitutes.

Serves 6

Cover the fish with the slices of pancetta and set aside until cooking time.

Heat a large nonstick ovenproof frying pan over high heat.

Add 1 Tbsp (15 mL) of the olive oil to the pan, toss in the carrots and snap peas, and let them sauté until they are nicely roasted and brown. Transfer to a baking sheet and set aside.

Heat the pan up again with 1 Tbsp (15 mL) olive oil; add the onions, mushrooms, asparagus, and red pepper. Maintain the heat on high and brown them well, about 5 to 8 minutes. Transfer to the baking sheet.

Heat the pan again with the remaining 2 Tbsp (30 mL) olive oil; add the potatoes and fry until browned and cooked. Add potatoes to the baking sheet with the carrots.

Heat the pan again on high heat and sear the fish about 3 minutes each side (adding oil if necessary, though the pancetta will naturally prevent sticking), and then place the pan, with the fish, into a 375°F (190°C) oven until the fish is cooked through, about 8 to 10 minutes.

While the fish is in the oven, heat a wok or large frying pan to high; add all the precooked vegetables plus the corn and toss until they are warm. Add the wine and the thyme leaves and toss.

To serve, divide the vegetables among six large rimmed dinner bowls. Place the fish on top and garnish with basil aioli.

- Six 6 oz (175 g) halibut fillets
- 24 slices pancetta
- 4 Tbsp (60 mL) olive oil, divided
- 24 baby carrots
- 24 snap peas
- 1 cup (250 mL) fresh or frozen pearl onions, peeled if fresh
- 10 button mushrooms, cut into sixths
- 12 spears asparagus, cut up or left whole
- 1 red pepper, cored and cut into strips
- 16 baby potatoes (fingerlings or red potatoes, chopped)
- One 10 oz (284 mL) can kernel corn, drained well
- ⅓ cup (80 mL) white wine
- 1 tsp (5 mL) fresh thyme
- Store-bought garlic aioli or Simple Basil Aioli (page 154) (garnish)

Wasabi and Panko–Crusted Halibut

This is one of my constant standbys. I love this recipe. Simple should be effortless, but it can also be elegant! Try substituting wild salmon or cod for the halibut.

Serves 4

Cut the fish into four equal serving pieces. Thinly spread the mayo on both sides of the fish. Dip into the panko crumbs, pressing them to adhere. Set fish aside.

Heat the oil in a nonstick ovenproof frying pan over medium heat. Fry the fish on both sides until crispy, then transfer to a preheated 400°F (200°C) oven for 8 to 10 minutes or until fish is cooked through.

Serve with Curry Sauce (page 158) and Forbidden Black Rice (page 135).

- 1½ lb (750 g) fresh halibut
- ½ cup (125 mL) wasabi mayonnaise
- 1 cup (250 mL) panko (Japanese breadcrumbs)
- 1 Tbsp (15 mL) grapeseed (or peanut) oil for frying

IN A PINCH

I like to finish all my fish dishes in the oven. Pan-searing the fish seals in the moisture, and the oven cooks it evenly without hot spots, giving you a perfect piece of fish every time.

Chef Michael Smith's Penne with Smoked Salmon and Cream Cheese Sauce

I have had the pleasure of interviewing Michael Smith several times for Global TV. As a cook, he is passionate and honest, and it comes through in his recipes. This dish stands out for me because it's so easy to make and it has incredible flavor. Seconds are a definite! Thank you, Chef.

Serves 4

Cook penne in lots of boiling salted water until al dente.

Scoop out some of the starchy cooking water and reserve. Drain the pasta but not quite all the way. Leave it a bit wet. Put the pasta back into the pot along with a splash or two of the reserved water.

While the pasta is still steaming hot, immediately add the rest of the ingredients except the salmon. Stir with a wooden spoon as the cheese melts and forms a creamy sauce.

At the last second, briefly stir in the smoked salmon; this way it won't break up as much. Season with salt and pepper and serve immediately.

- ▸ 1 lb (500 g) penne
- ▸ 1 cup (250 mL) cream cheese, softened
- ▸ 1 bunch fresh dill, chopped
- ▸ 4 green onions, thinly sliced
- ▸ ¼ cup (60 mL) capers
- ▸ Zest and juice of 1 lemon
- ▸ 1 Tbsp (15 mL) Dijon mustard
- ▸ 8 oz (250 g) smoked salmon (or more), cut into ribbons
- ▸ Sea salt
- ▸ Freshly ground pepper

IN A PINCH

You can use any of your favorite shaped pastas for this dish, like bowties; however, ribbon pastas, like spaghetti, don't work as well. This dish also works equally well with any kind of smoked fish. And if you don't have green onions, try a finely minced red onion. If you don't have capers, try a spoonful of standard green hot-dog relish.

Pork Cashew Stir-Fry

A satisfying stir-fry that is full of Asian flair, with a nice finish of cashews for crunch. I like to line the serving platter with steamed rice and pour the stir-fry overtop.

Serves 6

Mix all the marinade ingredients in a bowl, and add the diced pork. Mix well to coat and let the mixture sit until you are ready to cook.

Heat 1 Tbsp (15 mL) of the oil over high heat in a heavy-bottomed wok. Stir-fry the marinated pork for about 5 minutes until it starts to cook through. Remove and set aside. Add the remaining 1 Tbsp (15 mL) of oil and sear the onion until it begins to brown.

Mix together the garlic, ginger, hoisin sauce, rice vinegar, soy sauce, and sesame oil; pour into the wok and let the mixture cook for 1 minute.

Add the mushrooms, reserved pork, and stock. Stir to mix through with the heat on high. Add the snow peas and peppers and stir-fry until the veggies are cooked but still crisp.

To serve, turn the stir-fry onto a platter, top with the cashews, and garnish with the cilantro. Serve with steamed rice.

Marinated Pork

- ¼ cup (60 mL) sherry
- 2 Tbsp (30 mL) soy sauce
- 1 Tbsp (15 mL) toasted sesame oil
- 2 Tbsp (30 mL) cornstarch
- 2 lb (1 kg) pork tenderloin, cut into ½-inch (1 cm) cubes

Stir-Fry

- 2 Tbsp (30 mL) grapeseed oil, divided
- 1 large onion, cut into large dice
- 3 cloves garlic, minced
- 2 Tbsp (30 mL) freshly minced ginger
- ⅓ cup (80 mL) hoisin sauce
- 2 Tbsp (30 mL) rice vinegar
- 2 Tbsp (30 mL) soy sauce
- 2 Tbsp (30 mL) toasted sesame oil
- ½ lb (250 g) button mushrooms, cut into quarters
- ⅓ cup (80 mL) beef stock
- ½ lb (250 g) snow peas
- 1 red pepper, cored and diced
- 1 yellow pepper, cored and diced
- 1 cup (250 mL) toasted cashews
- ½ cup (125 mL) chopped fresh cilantro (garnish)

Rolled and Stuffed Chicken Breasts

I find that chicken, especially chicken breasts, can often border on *ho hum*. They tend to dry out and become tasteless. Here I use pancetta to really give this dish a kick, and a great sun-dried tomato paste that comes in squeeze tubes. Simple and effortless.

Serves 4 to 6

Lay the chicken on your work surface and pound it evenly to ¼-inch (6 mm) thickness.

Lay half of the cheese sticks along one end of one breast. Squeeze a thin line of tomato paste alongside the cheese, and place half the basil leaves on top. Roll the chicken up, jelly-roll fashion. Wrap the entire roll in pancetta and secure with toothpicks. Repeat with the other chicken breast. Refrigerate until ready to cook.

Sear the chicken in a medium-hot ovenproof frying pan until crispy on all sides. Transfer to a preheated 375°F (190°C) oven for about 20 minutes until the internal temperature of the chicken reaches 180°F (82°C).

Serve with 15-Minute Gorgonzola Pasta Sauce (page 160).

- 2 large boneless, skinless chicken breasts, preferably free-range
- 8 oz (250 g) Asiago or Swiss cheese, cut into long match-sticks, about ¼-inch wide
- ¼ cup (60 mL) sun-dried tomato paste
- 12 large fresh basil leaves
- 6 oz (175 g) thinly sliced pancetta
- Toothpicks to secure

IN A PINCH

You can roll up these chicken breasts several hours ahead of your dinner, or even the night before.

Chicken Pot Pie

I used to hate pot pie for the simple reason that bits of chicken skin and fat always found their way to my plate. I've solved this problem by cleaning my chicken perfectly so that every bite is simply yummy. These pies are freezer friendly. I like to double this up and freeze half for the days that I just don't feel like cooking. As an option, use individual onion soup bowls instead of one large gratin dish.

Serves 6 to 8

Roll out the puff pastry until it fits the size of your baking dish; set aside.

Heat the butter in a large saucepan over medium-low heat. Add the shallots and garlic; cook for about 2 minutes until soft. Add the flour and cook for a further 2 minutes, and then whisk in the milk until the sauce is smooth.

When smooth, add the chicken stock, cheese, herbs, and paprika (if using). Whisk until smooth and set aside.

Heat the olive oil in a nonstick frying pan. Brown the onions in a medium saucepan over high heat for about 5 minutes. Add the mushrooms; cook until soft, then toss in the chopped chicken, peas, and carrots. Combine with the cheese sauce, stir, and season to taste with sea salt and pepper.

Pour the mixture into a 6-cup (1.5 L) gratin dish, top with the rolled puff pastry and brush with a lightly beaten egg. Or divide the chicken mixture among individual onion soup bowls and top each with a round of pastry (as shown).

Bake in a preheated 375°F (190°C) oven for 12 minutes, or until the puff pastry is golden.

IN A PINCH

Use bagged, prewashed baby carrots and just blanch them for a minute before using them in the recipe. And I almost always use frozen pearl onions—who has time to peel fresh ones?

I generally roast a chicken every 10 days. We seldom finish it off, so I put the leftover meat in a freezer bag and keep adding to it. Within three weeks I have accumulated enough roasted chicken to do a batch of pot pies.

- 1 sheet of frozen puff pastry, thawed
- ¼ cup (60 mL) unsalted butter
- 2 large shallots, chopped
- 2 cloves garlic, minced
- ⅔ cup (160 mL) unbleached all-purpose flour
- 2 cups (500 mL) milk
- 2 cups (500 mL) chicken stock
- 1 cup (250 mL) grated Gruyère
- 2 Tbsp (30 mL) chopped Italian parsley
- 1 Tbsp (15 mL) fresh thyme or 1 tsp (5 mL) dried
- 1 Tbsp (15 mL) fresh tarragon or 1 tsp (5 mL) dried
- 1 tsp (5 mL) smoked Spanish paprika (optional)
- 2 Tbsp (30 mL) olive oil
- 20 fresh or frozen pearl onions or silverskin onions, peeled if fresh
- 2 cups (500 mL) quartered button mushrooms
- 4 cups (1 L) cooked and chopped chicken meat (all skin and bones removed)
- 1½ cups (375 mL) frozen sweet baby peas
- 1 cup (250 mL) peeled and chopped carrots
- Sea salt
- Freshly ground pepper
- 1 egg, lightly beaten

Beer Can Chicken

Everything may look perfect in a cookbook, but as you know, real life is not always like that. Take for example the dinner party that was also this cookbook's photo shoot. I took the beer can chicken, lathered it with barbecue sauce, and put it over direct heat. BIG MISTAKE. Less than 10 minutes later we began to smell something . . . To my horror, the chicken was *completely* charred. And guests were arriving in half an hour—talk about a real life pinch! Tammi, the hostess, happened to have a frozen chicken, so we defrosted it quickly and got it onto the barbecue. We did serve the blackened chicken in the end—it actually tasted great (once you scraped the burnt parts away). I say make the best of disaster. At least it tells a good story.

Serves 6

- ▸ 3 lb (1.5 kg) whole roasting chicken, preferably free-range
- ▸ 12 oz (355 mL) can medium to heavy beer
- ▸ 3-inch (8 cm) sprig fresh rosemary
- ▸ 3-inch (8 cm) sprig fresh thyme
- ▸ 2 bay leaves
- ▸ 1 tsp (5 mL) whole peppercorns
- ▸ 1 Tbsp (15 mL) olive oil
- ▸ ⅓ cup (80 mL) your favorite dry rub or barbecue sauce

Wash and dry the chicken, and remove the neck or giblets if they are inside the cavity. Preheat the barbecue to medium-high heat.

Open the beer, discard the pop tab, and pour out one-third of the beer. Insert the rosemary, thyme, bay leaves, and peppercorns into the can.

Rub the chicken with the olive oil and then pat the barbecue rub or sauce all over. Hold the chicken upright and sit it onto the beer can, pulling the legs forward so it looks like it is sitting. Place the whole thing onto a little pan.

Barbecue on indirect heat with the lid down for about 1½ hours until the internal temperature of the chicken is 180°F (82°C) and the skin is dark brown and crispy.

Take care when removing the chicken because the beer can is hot and so is the beer. Then have a good belly laugh with your friends seeing the chicken sitting spread-eagled atop the beer can looking like the king of the barbecue!

IN A PINCH

If you use barbecue sauce, check on the chicken more often as a sauced chicken has a tendency to burn. Remember, the first ingredient of barbecue sauce is usually sugar; the first ingredient of rubs is salt.

Joyce's Beef Chili

Joyce Ross has worked with us at the Gourmet Warehouse (my shop in Vancouver) for almost 10 years. She has earned the title of Store Gramma. I do not mean this in any way but good. She is the go-to person when you need understanding, sympathy, time off, but most importantly, lunch. We usually celebrate birthdays at the store with cake, but if Joyce is working on your birthday, you might get one of her incredible lunches: lasagna (my personal favorite), cabbage rolls, no-peek chicken, and, most recently, this chili recipe. She claims everything is simple, easy, and, most importantly, no fuss. She's right!

Serves 8

Lay enough aluminum foil on your work surface to enclose the meat completely. Place the beef on the foil and sprinkle the dry soup mix on both sides. Rub in the mix and seal the foil. Wrap an additional piece of foil around this so that it is sealed tight.

Place the wrapped beef on a baking sheet and bake in a preheated 325°F (160°C) oven for 3 hours.

Heat the olive oil in a 4-quart (4 L) Dutch oven; add the onions and sauté until they are brown and caramelized. Stir in the beans with the liquid along with the undiluted tomato soup and the chili powder. Cover and bake in a preheated 325°F (160°C) oven for 2 hours.

When the meat is done, remove from the foil, discard any liquid, and let the meat cool just long enough for you to comfortably handle it. When cooled, shred the meat and discard any visible fat.

Remove the beans from the oven and stir the meat into the bean mixture. Heat through and serve with grated cheese on top.

- 2 lb (1 kg) chuck steak, cut into 1-inch (2.5 cm) cubes
- One 1 oz (30 g) pkg Lipton onion soup mix
- 2 Tbsp (30 mL) olive oil
- 2 cups (500 mL) finely chopped yellow onion
- Three 19 oz (540 mL) cans kidney beans, undrained and unrinsed
- Two 10 oz (284 mL) undiluted cans tomato soup
- 3 Tbsp (45 mL) chili powder
- Grated Monterey Jack or cheddar cheese (garnish)

Anna Olson's Rockwell Bake

I have had the great pleasure of interviewing Anna Olson several times on my Saturday Chef's segment on Global TV's *Weekend Morning News*. This is her recipe, and it has rapidly become one of my favorites, not only because it tastes fantastic, but God knows we need more than soup recipes to use up the holiday turkey! Thank you for this, Anna.

Serves 6 to 8

Preheat the oven to 350°F (180°C). Grease a 9-inch (2.5 L) springform pan and place on a baking sheet.

Heat the oil in a frying pan over medium heat for a minute; add the onion, celery, and carrot. Sauté until the onions are translucent, about 5 minutes. Add the garlic and herbs and sauté 1 minute more. Add the cranberries and vermouth (or water) and simmer until almost all the liquid has evaporated. Remove from heat and cool to room temperature.

While the vegetables are cooling, whisk the eggs in a very large bowl, and then whisk in milk, mustard, salt, and pepper. Add bread cubes; toss to coat and let soak for 15 minutes, stirring occasionally.

Stir the cooled vegetables and diced turkey into the bread mixture, and then stir in 2 cups (500 mL) of the Swiss cheese. Spoon mixture into the prepared springform pan and sprinkle with the remaining ½ cup (125 mL) of Swiss cheese.

Bake for 1 hour until the top is a rich golden brown and the center springs back when pressed. Let rest for 15 minutes before unmolding to serve.

- 2 Tbsp (30 mL) olive oil for sautéing
- 1 cup (250 mL) finely diced onion
- 1 cup (250 mL) finely diced celery, including leaves
- ½ cup (125 mL) finely diced carrot
- 1 clove garlic, minced
- 1 Tbsp (15 mL) finely chopped fresh sage
- 2 tsp (10 mL) finely chopped fresh thyme
- 1 cup (250 mL) dried cranberries
- ¼ cup (60 mL) dry vermouth (or water)
- 5 large eggs
- 3 cups (750 mL) 2% milk
- 1 tsp (5 mL) Dijon mustard
- 1½ tsp (7 mL) fine sea salt
- ¼ tsp (1 mL) ground black pepper
- 8 cups (2 L) cubed day-old bread (white, whole wheat, or a mix) (1-inch/2.5 cm cubes)
- 3 cups (750 mL) cubed cooked turkey meat (½-inch/1 cm cubes)
- 2½ cups (625 mL) grated Swiss cheese, divided

Barbecued Duck Pizza

I suggest you purchase already-barbecued duck from a Chinese restaurant or Asian supermarket; you'll pay less, and you won't have a roasting pan to clean up.

Serves 6 to 8

For the dough, dissolve the sugar in the warm water. Sprinkle the yeast overtop and let it sit for 3 to 5 minutes until it begins to bubble and foam.

Place the flour and salt in the bowl of a food processor; add the yeast mixture and sesame oil. Turn the machine on and let it run while slowly pouring the ¾ cup (185 mL) water through the feed tube. The dough will form a ball on the side of the bowl.

Remove and knead lightly, just 2 minutes or so, until it is smooth and elastic. Place the dough in a bowl lightly oiled with half the grapeseed oil, lightly oil the top of the dough with the remaining oil, and let it rest until it doubles in size.

Lightly oil an 11-× 17-inch (28 × 42 cm) baking sheet and press the dough evenly into the pan. For the topping, combine the hoisin sauce, oil, ginger, and sambal oelek in a small bowl. Brush evenly over the pizza dough. Mix the two cheeses together in another bowl. Evenly spread the shredded duck meat, cilantro, sesame seeds, mushrooms, green onions, and cheese mixture, in that order, over the pizza.

Bake in a preheated 450°F (230°C) oven for about 15 minutes until the crust is golden, the cheese is bubbly, and the edges brown.

IN A PINCH

Buy prepared pizza dough from your local gourmet shop or super-market. That and the already-cooked duck (a roasted chicken from the supermarket works just as well!), and you have a quick and easy gourmet meal even the kids will love.

Of course you can use pizza pans and make these pizzas round, but rectangular is how I've always enjoyed pizza in Italy!

Pizza Dough

- 2 tsp (10 mL) sugar
- ½ cup (125 mL) warm water
- 1 Tbsp (15 mL) quick-rise yeast (1 envelope)
- 3 cups (750 mL) unbleached all-purpose flour
- 1 tsp (5 mL) sea salt
- 3 Tbsp (45 mL) toasted sesame oil
- ¾ cup (185 mL) warm water
- 2 Tbsp (30 mL) grapeseed oil

Topping

- ¼ cup (60 mL) hoisin sauce
- 2 Tbsp (30 mL) grapeseed oil
- 1 Tbsp (15 mL) freshly minced ginger
- 1 tsp (5 mL) sambal oelek (or any hot chili paste)
- 1 cup (250 mL) grated mozzarella cheese
- 1 cup (250 mL) grated Monterey Jack
- ½ barbecued duck, skinned, deboned, and shredded
- ½ cup (125 mL) chopped fresh cilantro
- 2 Tbsp (30 mL) toasted sesame seeds
- 1 cup (250 mL) fresh shiitake mushrooms, julienned
- 4 green onions, thinly sliced

Chipotle Chili
with Black and White Beans

This is a supereasy veggie chili that can be made in less than 30 minutes. I use store-bought salsa and canned beans to hasten the cooking. It may be hard to imagine an amazing-tasting chili in half an hour, but you have to try this. What's holding you back?

Serves 6

Heat the oil in a large 8-quart (9 L) soup pot; add the onion, garlic, celery, carrot, corn, and jalapeño (if using). Sauté until the veggies are soft and light brown.

Add the paprika, chili powder, cumin, and both kinds of beans, including the liquid in the cans. Stir in the stock and let the mixture cook for about 5 minutes. Add the salsa and cilantro and simmer for an additional 15 minutes.

Ladle the chili into ovenproof bowls, generously spread the Jack cheese overtop of each bowl, and broil until bubbly.

To serve, sprinkle the crumbled tortilla chips overtop, just before serving.

IN A PINCH

If you prefer a meatier chili, add 1 lb (500 g) of ground hamburger, turkey, or chicken. Fry until nicely browned and add to the chili just before you add the stock.

I always seem to have one-half-full or one-third-full jars of salsa, or jars with just a smidge left, hibernating in my fridge. Is it the same with you? Combine them all and toss into your chili!

- ¼ cup (60 mL) olive oil
- 1 large onion, diced
- 2–3 cloves garlic, minced
- 1 stalk celery, diced
- 1 large carrot, diced
- 1 cup (250 mL) frozen kernel corn, thawed
- ½ small jalapeño pepper, finely diced (optional)
- 2 Tbsp (30 mL) smoked Spanish paprika
- 2 Tbsp (30 mL) chili powder
- 2 tsp (10 mL) ground cumin
- One 19 oz (540 mL) can red kidney beans, undrained and unrinsed
- One 19 oz (540 mL) can white kidney beans, undrained and unrinsed
- 1 cup (250 mL) chicken (or vegetable) stock
- One 14 oz (398 mL) jar of your favorite salsa
- ½ bunch fresh cilantro, chopped
- 2 cups (500 mL) grated Monterey Jack
- 2 cups (500 mL) plain tortilla chips, crumbled (garnish)

Beef Tenderloin and Pasta

I use tenderloin so I can get this dish done in 20 minutes. You could also substitute slices of New York strip loin, pork tenderloin, or chicken breast for the tenderloin.

Serves 4

Cook pasta in boiling salted water until al dente.

While the pasta is cooking, heat the oil in a large frying pan; add the onions and cook on medium heat until they begin to soften. Add the garlic and the cubes of meat; increase the heat to high and toss for 5 to 8 minutes.

When the meat is almost cooked, add the sliced mushrooms and cook another 2 minutes.

Add the thyme, chili paste, stock paste, and tomatoes. Turn the heat down to medium and stir for 4 to 5 minutes until the tomatoes just begin to break up and release their juices.

Stir in the artichoke pieces and olives. Pour in the cream and let the sauce simmer on low for a few minutes. The sauce will begin to thicken up. Season with salt and pepper to taste and pour over the hot, cooked pasta.

- 1 lb (500 g) your favorite dry pasta
- 3 Tbsp (45 mL) olive oil
- 1 cup (250 mL) diced yellow onion
- 1 large clove garlic, minced
- 2 cups (500 mL) cubed beef tenderloin
- 5 large button mushrooms, sliced
- 2 tsp (10 mL) fresh thyme
- 1 Tbsp (15 mL) chili paste
- 2 Tbsp (30 mL) undiluted beef stock paste
- 15 cherry tomatoes, or 2 whole tomatoes, diced
- 6 jarred or canned artichokes, cut into sixths
- 10 kalamata olives, pitted
- ½ cup (125 mL) whipping cream
- Sea salt
- Freshly ground pepper

IN A PINCH

Everyone needs gourmet recipes that take less than a half hour to make. That's right—less than a half hour. This recipe and the next one are those recipes.

Grilled Organic Sausage with Stir-Fried Veggies

I love this midweek dinner. If you roast the garlic beforehand, this dish can be prepared in less than 30 minutes—the ultimate shortcut!

Serves 6 to 8

To roast garlic, cut ¼ inch (6 mm) off the top of the garlic heads; rub with oil, wrap loosely in foil, and bake for 1 hour in a preheated 325°F (160°C) oven until the garlic is soft and golden brown. Cool and remove papery skin. Set aside.

Heat the oil in a large saucepan; cook the onion until it just begins to turn brown. Add the peppers and asparagus and cook on high until both vegetables are golden. Transfer to a bowl and set aside.

Add the sausage pieces to the same pan and brown well on all sides. Add the potatoes and mushrooms along with the Marsala (or sherry) and sauté until the mushrooms are cooked through.

Toss the reserved vegetables back into the pan along with the roasted garlic cloves; drizzle with the lemon-infused oil (or regular olive oil) and balsamic vinegar, and season with the salt and pepper to taste.

Garnish with fresh basil and serve with basmati rice or buttered egg noodles.

IN A PINCH

Sausage used to be one kind, of one flavor, and made only from pork! But now chicken, duck, lamb, and even wild boar all have entered the arena, providing a variety of flavor profiles. Take your pick—they're all good.

- ▸ 2 whole heads garlic
- ▸ Olive oil for roasting garlic
- ▸ 2–3 Tbsp (30–45 mL) olive oil for sautéing
- ▸ 1 large onion, cut into large dice
- ▸ 3 red peppers, cored and cut into large dice
- ▸ 15 spears asparagus, cut into 2-inch (5 cm) pieces
- ▸ 10 fresh organic sausages, cut into ½-inch (1 cm) pieces
- ▸ 6 baby potatoes, cooked and cut into quarters
- ▸ 3 cups (750 mL) fresh shiitake mushrooms, cut into quarters
- ▸ ½ cup (125 mL) Marsala (or sweet sherry)
- ▸ ½ cup (125 mL) lemon-infused olive oil (page 67) (or regular olive oil)
- ▸ 2 Tbsp (30 mL) aged balsamic vinegar
- ▸ Sea salt
- ▸ Freshly ground pepper
- ▸ ½ cup (125 mL) fresh basil leaves, torn (garnish)

Veal Ragout

This is one of my favorite dishes to serve when feeding a crowd. The roasted chestnuts and pearl onions distinguish this dish and put it into the category of fantastic. The extra steps make it so worth the effort.

Serves 6 to 8

Pour the flour into a Ziploc bag; in three batches, add the veal cubes and shake until the cubes are evenly coated with the flour. Make sure you shake off the excess flour. Place some of the oil and butter in a frying pan on medium-high, and fry the veal cubes (in batches) until browned on all sides. Transfer the cubes to a large Dutch oven. Add the garlic, onions, chicken stock, thyme, and bay leaves. Bring to a boil, and then reduce the heat to a simmer. Cover and place in the preheated 350°F (180°C) oven for 1½ hours.

While the veal is in the oven, heat the 1 Tbsp (15 mL) oil and 1 Tbsp (15 mL) butter in a large frying pan. Add the pearl onions and shake the onions around until they begin to brown. Add the brown sugar to promote caramelization. Add the chestnuts along with the wine and simmer 8 to 10 minutes until the chestnuts are tender (easily pierced with a fork) and absorb the wine.

When the veal is done, pick out the garlic cloves and set aside. Remove the chunks of cooking onions, thyme sprigs, and bay leaves, and discard. Place the garlic cloves into a small bowl and smash them into a smooth paste.

Stir the garlic paste back into the veal juices; add the cream, plus the chestnut mixture, and stir to combine. Season with sea salt and pepper to taste.

Pour the veal into a deep serving bowl, garnish with the chopped parsley, and serve hot with your favorite cooked pasta.

- ½ cup (125 mL) unbleached all-purpose flour
- 4 lb (1.8 kg) veal shoulder, cubed
- ¼ cup (60 mL) olive oil, divided, for frying veal
- ¼ cup (60 mL) unsalted butter, divided, for frying veal
- 16 cloves garlic, peeled and left whole
- 2 small cooking onions, cut into quarters
- 2 cups (500 mL) chicken stock
- 2 sprigs fresh thyme
- 2 bay leaves
- 1 Tbsp (15 mL) olive oil
- 1 Tbsp (15 mL) unsalted butter
- 25 small pearl onions (thawed if frozen, peeled if fresh)
- 1 Tbsp (15 mL) brown sugar
- 20 whole natural roasted chestnuts (jarred or fresh)
- ½ cup (125 mL) red wine
- 1 cup (250 mL) whipping cream
- Sea salt
- Freshly ground pepper
- ½ cup (125 mL) minced parsley (garnish)

IN A PINCH

To roast fresh chestnuts, cut an X on the flat side of the chestnut. Place on a baking sheet and roast for 30 minutes in a preheated 375°F (190°C). Let the chestnuts cool slightly before peeling. A great shortcut is to buy jarred natural chestnuts from a good gourmet store.

Grilled Chili-Lime Pork Tenderloin

The other white meat, as pork has become known, delivers a great source of protein while allowing you to introduce any flavor trend that suits your taste. Pork tenderloin can be served with soba noodles or cellophane noodles, or on top of a mixed veggie stir-fry. This chili-lime dressing is supereasy because it uses staple condiments.

Serves 6 to 8

Trim the pork of any visible fat and place in a large Ziploc bag.

Mix together the garlic, chili paste, sesame oil, vinegar, soy sauce, lime zest, lime juice, and honey. Whisk well, then slowly pour in the oil, whisking until emulsified.

Pour half of this dressing into the Ziploc bag, reserving the other half. Press to seal the bag shut and let the pork marinate for 30 minutes or so.

Heat up your grill pan, frying pan, or barbecue to high; remove pork from the bag and sear on all sides. Continue to cook for 10 to 15 minutes, until desired doneness.

Let the pork rest for 10 minutes before slicing on the diagonal. Toss the cooked noodles in the reserved dressing, and serve with the pork. Garnish with sesame seeds, lime wedges, and cilantro.

- Pork tenderloins, 2½–3 lb (1.25–1.5 kg) in total
- 2 cloves garlic, minced
- 6 Tbsp (90 mL) chili paste
- ¼ cup (60 mL) toasted sesame oil
- ¼ cup (60 mL) rice vinegar
- ¼ cup (60 mL) soy sauce
- 1 Tbsp (15 mL) lime zest
- 2 Tbsp (30 mL) fresh lime juice
- 1 Tbsp (15 mL) liquid honey
- 1 cup (250 mL) grapeseed oil
- 1 lb (500 g) soba noodles (cooked al dente)
- ⅓ cup (80 mL) toasted sesame seeds (garnish)
- Lime wedges (garnish)
- ½ bunch fresh cilantro leaves (garnish)

IN A PINCH

Note that you can use any marinade on the shelf to marinate tenderloin. If you want a flavor profile similar to the above, use an Asian rub instead.

Deb's Ribs

Good ribs are hard to come by; they are often fatty and, at other times, dry and tough. This is an amazing recipe passed on to me by my cousin Debbie Whitehead in Calgary. At first, I was in disbelief that it could be so tasty and so easy. Funny how a little jar of VH sauce you can find in any grocery store can do so much! A toast to good condiments and a thank-you to Debbie. Once the ribs are boiled, it really comes down to pour and bake. How good is that?

Serves 6

Stud the four onion halves with the cloves. Place the onions, whole peppercorns, bay leaves, and carrots in a large stockpot; add enough water to come to the halfway mark. Bring to a boil; add the ribs and simmer for 45 to 60 minutes.

When done, remove the ribs from the pot, discarding the water and vegetables. Lay the ribs in a deep roasting pan. Pour the three jars of sparerib sauce overtop.

Cover with foil and bake in a preheated 350°F (180°C) oven for about 2 hours. Remove the foil, turn the ribs, and bake 1 hour more until the ribs fall from the bone.

Remove and transfer to a serving platter and garnish with the toasted sesame seeds, and green onions and fresh herbs (if using).

- 2 boiling onions, halved
- 12 whole cloves
- 2 Tbsp (30 mL) whole black peppercorns
- 6 bay leaves
- 2 carrots, peeled and chopped
- 4 racks of baby back ribs, cut into thirds
- Two 12 oz (340 mL) jars VH medium sparerib sauce
- One 12 oz (340 mL) jar VH Strong Garlic Rib Sauce
- ⅔ cup (160 mL) toasted sesame seeds (garnish)
- 1 bunch green onions, thinly sliced (optional garnish)
- Sprigs of fresh herbs, such as rosemary (optional garnish)

Lamb Tagine

A tagine is a large glazed earthenware cooking vessel with a tall conical lid. It is traditionally used to prepare the simmered dish of the same name. Condensation on the lid falls onto the dish and keeps it perfectly moist. The tagine pot is not essential; instead you can use an enameled or cast iron casserole with a lid.

Serves 4 to 6

Mix all the spices together and rub over the lamb cubes. Let the lamb sit for about 15 minutes to absorb the flavor of the rub.

While the lamb is resting, heat your tagine or heavy-bottomed casserole to medium-high heat on the stovetop. Add the butter and oil, and then the onion, and sauté for about 5 minutes.

Add the seasoned lamb along with the garlic. Brown well on all sides. Add water (or stock) to the tagine. Cover and place in a preheated 375°F (190°C) oven for about 30 minutes. Lift the lid and check the liquid level, adding more water or stock if necessary. Stir. Add the figs and chopped lemon. Put the lid back on and cook for another 15 minutes, just until the lamb is fork tender.

Serve with Vegetable Couscous (page 134) and harissa.

- 2 Tbsp (30 mL) smoked Spanish paprika
- 2 tsp (10 mL) saffron threads, pounded into a powder
- 2 tsp (10 mL) ground fennel seeds
- 1 tsp (5 mL) ground ginger
- 1 tsp (5 mL) ground cumin
- 1 tsp (5 mL) ground cinnamon
- 1 tsp (5 mL) ground turmeric
- 2 lb (1 kg) lamb sirloin, cut into 1-inch (2.5 cm) cubes
- 2 Tbsp (30 mL) unsalted butter
- 2 Tbsp (30 mL) olive oil
- 2 large onions, diced
- 2–3 cloves garlic, minced
- 1 cup (250 mL) water (or stock)
- 2 cups (500 mL) dried Black Mission figs, cut into quarters
- ½ preserved lemon, rind finely chopped (pulp discarded)

IN A PINCH

Homemade spice mixtures are terrific but take a bit of time. Good store-bought rubs are easy to source and make your life just a bit easier. For tagines, I like NoMU Moroccan Rub.

Braised Lamb Shanks

My colleague and superb cooking teacher Glenys Morgan makes the best lamb shanks I have tasted. Her method of an "overnight rub rest" is a good one; I once again take the short road/streamline the prep by applying a premade rub. I love using my Le Creuset pot for this dish.

Serves 6

Rub the shanks with the spice rub, ensuring that you cover all surfaces. Refrigerate overnight.

The next day, place the seasoned shanks in a on a large parchment-lined baking sheet and roast in a preheated 425°F (220°C) oven for about 30 minutes, turning to ensure even browning on all sides.

While the shanks are roasting, heat the oil in a large Dutch oven. Stir in the onion, garlic, paprika, and saffron, and sauté for 8 minutes until soft but not brown.

Pour in the stock; bring to a boil, and add the roasted shanks. Cover with parchment so that the parchment is touching the lamb. Place the lid on the pot and cook in a preheated 325°F (160°C) oven for 2 hours.

Remove the shanks from the pot, set aside, strain the sauce, and pour over the shanks.

I like to serve this with Vegetable Couscous (page 134).

- 6 meaty lamb shanks
- 5 Tbsp (75 mL) Moroccan rub
- 2 Tbsp (30 mL) olive oil
- 1 large onion, peeled and diced
- 4 cloves garlic, minced
- 1 Tbsp (15 mL) smoked Spanish paprika (hot)
- 2 pinches of saffron threads, pounded into a powder
- 3 cups (750 mL) chicken (or veal) stock

IN A PINCH

You don't have to use Moroccan rub — it can be any kind of rub you like.

5 Quick & Easy Ways with Filo

Filo is one of the most versatile pastries with which to work. It's cost effective and can also be used in both sweet and savory applications. Here are some different ways I like to use what I call a Great Gift of Boxed Pastry.

1   Filo pizza
    Place a layer of filo on a baking sheet. Brush lightly with olive oil and sprinkle with Parmesan cheese. Top with another sheet, brush with oil, and sprinkle with more cheese. Repeat with four more sheets. Working quickly, top the filo with two or three of your favorite toppings. Don't overload it! I like to use thinly sliced sweet onions, sliced Roma tomatoes, fresh herbs, grated Swiss or Jack cheese, pitted olives, or pesto. Bake for 15 to 20 minutes at 375°F (190°C).

2   Filo-wrapped asparagus
    Blanch 16 spears of asparagus for 2 minutes, and drop into ice water. Dry on paper towels. Stack four sheets of filo together and then cut into quarters, and stack together (you should have stack of 16 pieces). Working one at time, from the top of the stack down, brush each square with olive oil, then spread with a thin smear of honey Dijon mustard. Place the asparagus spear on one end of each of the filo rectangles and roll up. Place seam side down on a baking sheet and lightly brush the tops of the filo with oil. Bake for 8 to 10 minutes at 375°F (190°C). Serve warm.

3   Filo baskets
    Lightly brush a sheet of filo with grapeseed oil, and then, depending on whether you're going to fill the baskets with sweet or savory filling, lightly sprinkle with sugar or Parmesan cheese. Place another sheet on top of the first and repeat. Place one last sheet overtop and brush with oil. Cut filo into 3- or 4-inch (8 or 10 cm) squares, and push into a muffin pan, pressing to the sides to keep the cavity open.

    Bake for 8 to 10 minutes at 375°F (190°C). Cool, and if going savory, fill with curried chicken or shrimp, or mixed mushrooms. If you're going sweet, fill with lemon curd, chocolate mousse, or fresh fruit with mascarpone or crème fraîche.

4   Sweet filo stacks

Use the same three-layer procedure as you did with the baskets (above) and use sugar to sprinkle in between the filo sheets. Cut into 3- or 4-inch (8 or 10 cm) squares. Lay the cut squares on a baking sheet, and bake for 8 to 10 minutes (or until the cups are golden brown) at 375°F (190°C). When they're cool, make little stacks! Layer the stacks with whipped cream, ice cream, or mascarpone, and your favorite fresh fruit. Repeat twice until your stack has three layers of each. Dust with icing sugar and/or Dutch cocoa powder.

5   Breakfast filo cups

Cut filo into 6-inch (15 cm) squares. Lightly brush a square with melted butter and sprinkle with Parmesan cheese. Layer one more square on top and repeat, using four squares in total, overlapping the squares so that they create an uneven edge, giving it a flower petal look. Fit the squares into a large muffin pan, pushing the filo against the sides with your fingers so that you have a large cup. Bake the filo cups in a preheated 375°F (190°C) oven for 6 to 8 minutes or until they are golden brown and crispy.

Make a scrambled egg filling by heating 2 Tbsp (30 mL) butter in a large nonstick frying pan; add three diced shallots and sauté for about 2 minutes. Add 1 cup (250 mL) sliced mushrooms and cook until done. Lightly beat six eggs with milk and pour into the pan. Cook until the eggs are about half-way cooked. Add smoked salmon or cooked shrimp, fresh dill, and feta and continue to cook until the eggs are done. Season with salt and pepper.

Spoon into the prepared filo cups and serve warm.

Sides

Blue Cornbread

Cornbread is the staple of the breadbasket in the Deep South. I love this recipe as an alternative to the overserved baguette. If you can't find corn salsa, use drained kernel corn in its place. Yellow cornmeal can be a substitute for the blue. Try this with chili.

Serves 6 to 8

Sift all the dry ingredients together in a large bowl and set aside.

Whisk together the buttermilk, sour cream, eggs, and butter in a medium bowl. Set aside.

Lightly oil a 10-inch (25 cm) square baking pan or cast iron frying pan.

Mix the wet ingredients into the dry, adding the corn salsa, and hot peppers (if using). Stir well. Spoon half the batter into the prepared pan, evenly sprinkle the cheese overtop, and then top with the remaining batter. Bake in a preheated 400°F (200°C) oven for 25 to 30 minutes until the cornbread is golden brown.

Cool, then remove from the pan, and enjoy it warm or at room temperature.

- 1 cup (250 mL) blue cornmeal
- 1 cup (250 mL) unbleached all-purpose flour
- 1 Tbsp (15 mL) baking powder
- 1 Tbsp (15 mL) sugar
- 1½ tsp (7 mL) sea salt
- 1 cup (250 mL) buttermilk
- ½ cup (125 mL) sour cream
- 2 large eggs, lightly beaten
- 5 Tbsp (75 mL) melted unsalted butter
- 1 cup (250 mL) corn salsa
- ½ cup (125 mL) chopped canned serrano (or jalapeño) peppers (optional)
- 1 cup (250 mL) grated Monterey Jack

IN A PINCH

Use a jar of spicy corn salsa to give the cornbread a kick.

Savory Bread Pudding

Bread pudding has always been associated with sweet endings. These days, when we pay upwards of $4 for those lovely country loaves that are generously studded with everything from fragrant herbs and imported cheeses to dried fruits and nuts, it is almost criminal to watch any uneaten pieces find their way to the bird feeder. This savory pudding is a great substitute for potatoes, rice, or noodles.

Serves 6 to 8

To roast garlic, cut ¼ inch (6 mm) off the top of the garlic head; rub with oil, wrap loosely in foil, and bake for 1 hour in a preheated 325°F (160°C) oven until the garlic is soft and golden brown. Cool and remove papery skin. Set aside.

Grease an 8-× 4-inch (1.5 L) loaf pan and set aside.

Whisk the eggs in a large bowl; add the milk, cheese, and mustard. Season with the salt and pepper to taste. Sauté the onion slices in grapeseed oil until golden. Add the cooked onion, crispy bacon, roasted garlic, and bread cubes to the egg mixture.

Toss well to evenly combine the ingredients. Pour into the prepared pan, top with the Parmesan, and bake for 45 minutes in a preheated 350°F (180°C) oven.

- 1 whole head garlic
- Olive oil for roasting garlic
- 3 large eggs, beaten
- 1½ cups (375 mL) whole milk
- 1 cup (250 mL) grated Swiss cheese of your choice
- 1 Tbsp (15 mL) Dijon mustard
- Sea salt
- Freshly ground pepper
- 1 medium onion, thinly sliced
- 1 Tbsp (15 mL) grapeseed oil for frying onion
- 6 slices bacon, chopped and fried until crispy
- 4 cups (1 L) cubed day-old bread
- ½ cup (125 mL) grated Parmesan cheese

Reggiano Cheese Sticks

Cheese and wine, wine and cheese—a combination that never fails to please. Turn the idea into an aromatic baked pastry-bound cheese stick paired with a perfectly balanced glass of heart-and-soul-warming wine. A match, I say.

Makes 24

Lay the puff pastry on a lightly floured work surface. Roll the dough out to about a ⅛-inch (3 mm) thickness.

Mix the grated cheese, smoked paprika, and salt together in a medium bowl. Spread over the puff. Carefully press your rolling pin over the cheese, ensuring that it adheres to the pastry.

Fold the pastry in half and roll back out to the original size. With a sharp knife or pizza cutter, cut ½-inch (1 cm) strips crosswise to make 24 strips. Pick up the strips, roll them in sesame seeds (if using), and twist strips to create cheese sticks.

Lay the sticks on a baking sheet lined with parchment paper. Bake in a preheated 400°F (200°C) oven for about 15 minutes until golden brown and crisp. Let cool.

To serve, transfer to a tall wine glass or highball glass, and enjoy with a glass of wine.

- 1 lb (500 g) frozen puff pastry, thawed
- 1 cup (250 mL) freshly grated Parmigiano Reggiano cheese
- 1 tsp (5 mL) sweet smoked Spanish paprika
- 1 tsp (5 mL) fleur de sel
- Black sesame seeds (optional)

Coconut-Infused Rice

Coconut-infused rice can be served with duck, pork, or fish for any celebratory feast.

Serves 6

Heat the oil in a wok over high heat; add the onion, garlic, and ginger. Toss the mixture together for about 4 minutes and then add rice. Toss well, and then pour in the stock, water, and coconut milk.

Bring to a boil and then reduce the heat to a simmer; cover tightly with lid until the liquid is absorbed.

To serve, stir in the green onion, lemongrass, and cilantro. Garnish with the chopped cashews and serve.

- 2 Tbsp (30 mL) grapeseed (or peanut) oil
- 1 medium yellow onion, diced
- 2 cloves garlic, thinly sliced
- 1-inch (5 cm) piece ginger, peeled and finely chopped
- 1½ cups (375 mL) short-grain white rice (uncooked)
- 1½ cups (375 mL) chicken (or vegetable) stock
- ¾ cup (185 mL) water
- ½ cup (125 mL) coconut milk
- 2 green onions, thinly sliced
- 1 stalk lemongrass (white part only), thinly sliced
- ¼ cup (60 mL) chopped fresh cilantro
- ½ cup (125 mL) chopped cashews (garnish)

Nasi Goreng

This classic Indonesian rice dish looks like a lot of work, but you can take many shortcuts. One is to buy packages of premade Nasi Goreng seasoning. (Asian Home Gourmet is a good brand.) Second is to steam the rice the day before. And third is to crisp the shallots several days beforehand. You can make a big batch and use it for several recipes in this book. Or you can buy them canned, from Denmark.

Serves 6

Bring the water and rice to a boil. Turn down to a simmer, cover tightly, and cook until the water is absorbed. Spoon into a large bowl and cover the rice with a damp cloth until it reaches room temperature.

While the rice is cooking, make the crispy shallot garnish. Dredge the shallots in flour, coating them evenly and shaking off the excess. Heat 1 Tbsp (15 mL) of the oil in a small saucepan; add the shallots and fry on medium heat, stirring until they are browned evenly. Remove and blot on paper towels to remove any excess oil. Set aside.

When the rice has cooled down, heat the remaining 3 Tbsp (45 mL) of oil in a wok over high heat; add the onion, garlic, ginger, and sambal oelek and sauté for about 2 minutes. Add the cabbage and prawns and stir-fry for about 5 minutes until the cabbage is slightly soft and the prawns bright pink.

Add the soy sauce and fish sauce; toss to combine and then stir in the cooked rice and mix until heated. Season with sea salt and pepper to taste.

Transfer to a serving dish, arrange the sliced cucumbers around the edge of the dish, and top with the crispy shallots.

- 2½ cups (625 mL) water
- 2 cups (500 mL) long-grain white rice
- 2 large shallots, sliced
- Unbleached all-purpose flour for dredging shallots
- 4 Tbsp (60 mL) grapeseed oil, divided
- 1 medium onion, diced
- 2 cloves garlic, minced
- 2 Tbsp (30 mL) freshly minced ginger
- 1 Tbsp (15 mL) sambal oelek
- 1 cup (250 mL) shredded napa cabbage
- ½ lb (250 g) fresh prawns (16/20 count), peeled and roughly chopped
- 2 Tbsp (30 mL) soy sauce
- 2 tsp (10 mL) fish sauce
- Sea salt
- Freshly ground pepper
- 1 cup (250 mL) thinly sliced Japanese (or English) cucumber (garnish)

Vegetable Couscous

You can serve this couscous as a side dish or as a salad. To give the couscous an extra boost of flavor, cook it in chicken or vegetable stock instead of water. I like to pair this recipe with the Braised Lamb Shanks (page 121) or the Brined and Grilled Prawns (page 89).

Serves 6

Bring the water (or stock) to boil; add the turmeric and turn off the heat.

Pour in the couscous and stir. Place the lid on the pot and let it sit for 5 to 8 minutes or until all the liquid has been absorbed by the couscous.

In the meantime, sauté the pearl onions over medium-high heat in olive oil, until golden brown. Mix all the dressing ingredients together, and pour over the couscous when it's done. Add the cucumbers, grape tomatoes, olives, red pepper, and pearl onions. Stir well and season with salt and pepper. (If using jarred red pepper, blot dry on paper towels before chopping.)

Garnish with the mint, cilantro, and pine nuts just before serving.

- 2 cups (500 mL) water (or chicken or vegetable stock)
- 1 tsp (5 mL) ground turmeric
- 1¾ cups (435 mL) couscous
- 1 cup (250 mL) frozen pearl onions (no need to thaw)
- 1 Tbsp (15 mL) olive oil
- 1 cup (250 mL) sliced and quartered Japanese cucumbers
- 1 cup (250 mL) grape tomatoes, halved
- ½ cup (125 mL) pitted kalamata olives
- 1 roasted red pepper (roasted yourself, or jarred), chopped
- Kosher salt
- Freshly ground pepper
- ¼ cup (60 mL) chopped fresh mint (garnish)
- ¼ cup (60 mL) chopped fresh cilantro (garnish)
- ⅓ cup (80 mL) toasted pine nuts (garnish)

Lemon Dressing
- ½ cup (125 mL) good-quality olive oil
- 3 Tbsp (45 mL) champagne vinegar
- 1 Tbsp (15 mL) Dijon mustard
- 1 clove garlic, minced
- 1 tsp (5 mL) finely chopped preserved lemon

Forbidden Black Rice

Centuries ago, Chinese Forbidden Black Rice was reserved exclusively for royalty. This exotic, color-intense rice is still prized for its medicinal and nutritional value. Substitute it in any rice dish and add a little royalty to your meals!

Serves 4 to 6

- ▸ 1½ cups (375 mL) water
- ▸ 1 cup (250 mL) Chinese Forbidden Black Rice
- ▸ Pinch of sea salt

Bring the water and rice to a boil. Turn down to a simmer, cover tightly, and cook until the water is absorbed and the rice is cooked through. Add a good pinch of salt and serve.

IN A PINCH

One cup (250 mL) of cubed fresh mango adds vibrant color and texture to the rice. Another option is to replace ¼ cup (60 mL) of the water called for in the recipe with the same amount of coconut milk and to add a good grating of fresh ginger.

Balsamic Roasted Pumpkin and Beets

Pumpkin is usually reserved for pies, soups, or loaf cakes. But there is so much more it can do. Roasting brings out the inherent natural sugars of pumpkin and gives it star status.

Serves 4 to 6

Place the cubed pumpkin and beets in a large bowl. Pour the oil and balsamic overtop, add the 2 tsp (10 mL) fleur de sel and ground pepper, and toss well to coat.

Transfer to a large rimmed baking sheet. Spread out into a single layer and bake in a preheated 375°F (190°C) oven for 50 to 60 minutes until golden brown and tender.

Transfer to a serving bowl and drizzle over a bit more olive oil and balsamic. Sprinkle the fresh thyme overtop, and garnish with the crumbed chèvre. Season with salt and pepper to taste.

IN A PINCH

France may have started the "salt revolution" with fleur de sel, which comes from the coast of Brittany and also from Normandy and the Camargue; but now countries like Portugal, Spain, and Italy are producing it too. Its superb taste makes it a great finishing salt.

Perhaps it is the sheer size of pumpkins that discourages anything but carving out faces for Halloween. You can buy pumpkin in pieces at most stores or simply choose the smallest one you can find.

- 2 lb (1 kg) piece of pumpkin, peeled and cut into 1-inch (2.5 cm) cubes
- 1 lb (500 g) beets, tops removed, peeled and cut into 1-inch (2.5 cm) cubes
- ½ cup (125 mL) olive oil
- ¼ cup (60 mL) balsamic vinegar
- 2 tsp (10 mL) fleur de sel for roasting
- Freshly ground pepper for roasting
- Olive oil for drizzling
- Balsamic vinegar for drizzling
- 1 Tbsp (15 mL) fresh thyme
- Crumbled chèvre or feta (garnish—I like to use a fair amount)
- Fleur de sel
- Freshly ground pepper

Asian Beet Salad

In a pinch, this salad can be prepared as quick as you can boil beets!

Serves 4

Boil the beets until they are cooked through and can be easily pierced with a knife. Drain, and place in a serving boil.

In a medium frying pan, heat together the sesame seeds, garlic, mustard, soy sauce, rice vinegar, and sesame oil. Whisk for a quick minute just until the garlic is cooked, then whisk in the grapeseed (or peanut) oil. Pour over the warm beets. Season with pepper.

Serve hot or at room temperature.

- 2 lb (1 kg) beets, tops removed, peeled, and cut into 1-inch (2.5 cm) cubes
- ⅓ cup (80 mL) sesame seeds
- 2 cloves garlic, minced
- 1 Tbsp (15 mL) Dijon mustard
- 1 Tbsp (15 mL) soy sauce
- 2 Tbsp (30 mL) rice vinegar
- 2 Tbsp (30 mL) toasted sesame oil
- ½ cup (125 mL) grapeseed (or peanut) oil
- Freshly ground pepper

Latkas, Tammi's Way

My good friend Tammi Kerzner makes the best latkas I have ever tasted. While she was showing me her technique of hand-grating the potato, I asked her if a food processor wouldn't make it easier. Brian, her husband, jumped in to say that if she used a processor, the latkas wouldn't come with the all-important guilt factor. The intense hand-grating deserves accolades, but you could deviate if guilt isn't your shtick! Enjoy Latkas, Tammi's Way, which she sometimes refers to as "The Genius's Latkas."

Makes 20

Combine the grated onion and potatoes together in a large bowl; mix in the lightly beaten egg. Sprinkle the flour overtop, along with the kosher salt and the pepper to taste. Mix with your hands. (The mixture will be a bit soupy.)

Heat the oil on medium-high heat in a large nonstick frying pan. Drop the potato mixture by ¼ cupfuls (60 mL) into the hot oil. Fry latkas 2 to 3 minutes on each side until completely browned.

Remove and drain on paper towels. Transfer to a baking sheet lined with parchment paper and keep warm in a preheated 250°F (120°C) oven until ready to serve. Serve with sour cream and applesauce.

- 1 yellow onion, grated on medium shred
- 6 russet potatoes, coarsely grated and squeezed dry to equal 6 cups (1.5 L)
- 1 large egg, lightly beaten
- ¼ cup (60 mL) unbleached all-purpose flour
- 1 Tbsp (15 mL) kosher salt
- Freshly ground pepper
- Enough canola oil to cover ¼ inch (6 mm) of your frying pan
- 1 cup (250 mL) sour cream (garnish)
- 1 cup (250 mL) applesauce (garnish)

IN A PINCH

You can also make the latkas 2 hours ahead of time and keep them warm in the oven.

Root Vegetable Purée
with Crispy Shallots

In all honesty, I've never really jumped for joy over strongly flavored vegetables like turnips, parsnips, or Brussels sprouts. The following recipe was a total revelation to me. It is truly an explosion of massive flavor that will change your opinion on strong-tasting root veggies. You must try this; I personally guarantee instant love.

Serves 6 to 8

Dredge the shallots in the flour, making sure to coat them all evenly. Shake off the excess flour and discard. Heat the oil in a medium saucepan; add the floured shallots and fry on medium heat, stirring until they are browned evenly. Remove and blot on paper towels to remove any excess oil. Set aside.

Boil the potato, turnips, and carrot in a large pot of salted boiling water until fork tender. Drain vegetables and place in the bowl of a food processor. Add the butter and cream and purée until smooth.

Transfer the mixture to a serving bowl and stir in the crispy shallots. Season with salt and pepper to taste and serve hot.

- 4 large shallots, sliced
- Unbleached all-purpose flour for dredging shallots
- 2 Tbsp (30 mL) olive oil
- 1 large russet potato, peeled and cubed
- 2 medium turnips, peeled and cubed
- 1 small carrot, peeled and cubed
- ⅓ cup (80 mL) unsalted butter
- ⅓ cup (80 mL) whipping cream
- Sea salt
- Freshly ground Tellicherry (or black) pepper

Gruyère Potatoes

One of my favorite cooking cheeses on the planet is Gruyère. The intense, nutty flavor makes almost everything cooked with it taste better—mushrooms for sure, and potatoes. This dish is so easy you can almost do it blindfolded. I always use a silicone muffin pan to make the cleanup easy.

Serves 6

Slice the potatoes fine using the slicing blade on a handheld mandoline (see page 165) or of a food processor.

Stir the pepper and nutmeg into the cream. If your large six-cup muffin pan is not silicone, butter it well. Place a few potato slices along with 2 tsp (10 mL) of the cream in each cup, followed by a thin layer of Gruyère. Continue layering until each is filled ¼ inch (6 mm) from the top.

Sprinkle the tops with Parmesan and bake in a preheated 375°F (190°C) oven for about 30 minutes until golden brown and bubbly.

Let the potatoes sit for 10 minutes to set, and then remove from pan and garnish with the chopped parsley (if using). Heavenly indulgence.

- ▸ 1 lb (500 g) small red (or fingerling) potatoes
- ▸ 1 tsp (5 mL) freshly ground pepper
- ▸ Pinch of ground nutmeg
- ▸ 1 cup (250 mL) whipping cream
- ▸ 8 oz (250 g) Gruyère, grated
- ▸ ½ cup (125 mL) grated Parmesan cheese
- ▸ ⅓ cup (80 mL) finely chopped parsley (optional garnish)

Crispy Yams

We are all familiar with yam fries, most often enjoyed in restaurants just because they seem to prepare them the best. I've been trying to duplicate restaurant-quality yam fries for a while, but I've ended up departing from the finger-fries version a bit. I dice yams into ½-inch (1 cm) cubes, toss with a dry rub, and pan-fry them in a bit of grapeseed oil. Voilà, crispy on the outside and buttery on the inside.

Serves 4 to 6

- 2 medium yams, peeled and cut into ½-inch (1 cm) cubes
- ½ cup (125 mL) Moroccan rub (or any other rub that you like)
- ½ cup (125 mL) grapeseed oil

Place yam cubes in a large Ziploc bag and add the rub. Shake well to coat.

Heat the oil in a shallow nonstick frying pan. Add the yam cubes and fry for 5 to 8 minutes until golden brown and tender.

Blot off the excess oil with paper towel and serve hot.

IN A PINCH

If you just want regular crispy yams, dismiss the rub and fry them plain; once they are cooked, simply sprinkle with sea salt and serve.

Pan-Roasted Spring Asparagus

Asparagus can be had in a variety of sizes: skinny and pencil thin, thick and fat, or right in the middle. To peel or not to peel is another chef's dilemma. (Personally, I never peel.) Whatever size you do choose, cook according to the thickness of the stalk, and snap the end of the stalk to ensure you've removed the tough bit. The tender asparagus is ready to steam, roast, or fry. In my opinion, roasting and frying bring out the best flavor.

Serves 4 to 6

Place the asparagus on a large rimmed baking sheet in a single layer. Drizzle with the olive oil, and season with the sel gris and pepper.

Place in a preheated 400°F (200°C) oven and roast for about 10 minutes (depending on the asparagus's thickness), shaking the pan halfway through. They should not be overcooked.

Remove from the pan, transfer to a serving platter, give the asparagus a squeeze of lemon juice, and garnish with the shavings of Parmesan cheese.

- 1 lb (500 g) asparagus
- 2 Tbsp (30 mL) extra virgin olive oil
- Sprinkle of sel gris (grey salt)
- Generous grind of a five-peppercorn blend
- Squeeze of fresh lemon juice
- ½ cup (125 mL) shaved Parmesan cheese (garnish)

IN A PINCH

Five-peppercorn blend is simply equal portions of black, white, green, and pink peppercorns, and a magical fifth, which is not pepper at all but whole allspice to lend aromatics to the blend.

Spicy Green Beans

More beans, please! With just a few simple ingredients, you can elevate the status of the simple green bean to *za za zoom*. This dish is truly one of my favorites and can be cooked in less than six minutes. You can use thin asparagus as an alternative to the beans.

Serves 4 to 6

Mix the soy sauce, chili paste, ginger, and garlic together in a small bowl. Set aside.

Heat a nonstick medium frying pan over high heat. Add the oil and swirl to coat. Toss in the beans and stir until they begin to crackle and brown, about 5 minutes.

Add the soy sauce mixture to the browned beans and toss to coat. Let the beans sauté in the mixture for about 1 minute before transferring to a serving platter and garnishing with the toasted sesame seeds.

- ¼ cup (60 mL) soy sauce
- ¼ cup (60 mL) chili paste
- 2 Tbsp (30 mL) freshly grated ginger
- 3 cloves garlic, minced
- 2 Tbsp (30 mL) grapeseed oil
- 1 lb (500 g) green beans, trimmed
- ⅓ cup (80 mL) toasted sesame seeds (garnish)

IN A PINCH

Choose the thinnest beans you can find. I always choose the French haricots verts when they are available. They cost a bit more, but they're worth it.

5 Quick & Easy Ways with Pancetta

We are all familiar with the saying "everything tastes better with bacon." And it's true: is there anything better than the smoky, salty crunch of a crisp piece of bacon? Well, yes: everything tastes better with pancetta! I prefer the Italians' version of bacon; it's not quite as salty or fatty, and when you get it sliced paper thin, it cooks up in minutes. You can also buy spicy pancetta. I always have a package of thinly sliced pancetta in the freezer for when I need it.

Here are five things I like to do with it:

1   Chop it up, sauté it with onions, and add it to a pasta sauce.

2   Wrap it around figs, asparagus, or large button mushrooms, and grill until crispy.

3   Fry it up crispy, and crumble it as a topping for salad, macaroni and cheese, or whenever you want to add crunch and salt.

4   Place several slices of pancetta between two sheets of parchment paper. Make sure the slices aren't touching each other. Lay this on a baking sheet and sandwich it by placing another baking sheet on top. Place in a 375°F (190°C) oven for about 10 minutes. You'll end up with perfectly crisp pancetta discs to use for garnishing salads or to serve with an egg dish.

5   Place pancetta slices on both sides of a pounded chicken breast. Pan-fry the chicken in a hot nonstick frying pan. The pancetta will adhere to the chicken, infusing it with flavor and sealing in the juices. Then deglaze the pan with a bit of Dijon mustard, white wine, and a bit of chicken stock. Pour this sauce over the pancetta-wrapped chicken. Voilà!

Sauces &
Marinades

Simple Basil Aioli

My daughter, Christina, is in love with this sauce. It makes everything from simple oven fries to halibut taste amazing. All you need is a mini Cuisinart or a high-powered blender to whiz this sauce into smooth perfection.

Makes 1 cup (250 mL)

Place the basil and garlic in the bowl of the food processor and purée. Add the mustard, lemon juice, and egg yolk. Purée until smooth; scrape down the sides of the bowl and pulse until the mixture is smooth.

With the motor running, slowly pour in the olive oil; the sauce will thicken. Season with salt and pepper to taste. Transfer to a serving bowl and refrigerate until serving.

- ▸ 2 heaping cups (500 mL+) fresh basil leaves, stems removed
- ▸ 2 large cloves garlic, peeled
- ▸ 1 heaping Tbsp (15 mL+) Dijon mustard
- ▸ Juice of ½ lemon
- ▸ 1 large egg yolk
- ▸ ⅔ cup (160 mL) good-quality extra virgin olive oil
- ▸ 1 tsp (5 mL) kosher salt
- ▸ Freshly ground pepper

IN A PINCH

This sauce keeps for five days, so if you plan ahead, it will be ready the day you want to use it.

My Favorite Asian Dressing

I used to be a flight attendant with Canadian Pacific Airlines. (Way back when! They have since been gobbled up by mergers and all those things that make the end of an era sad.) During my flying years, I took up the opportunity to travel the globe and attend elite cooking schools. One of my *stages*—a cheffy term for an "internship"—was in Japan. *Simple* defines Japan's cuisine perfectly, with attention paid to the marriage of just a few ingredients to achieve perfection. I love this dressing so much that I often double it up.

Makes 1 cup (250 mL)

Mix together the garlic, mustard, soy sauce, vinegar, and pepper in a small bowl. Slowly pour in the oil while whisking all the time until the dressing comes together in a creamy, smooth consistency. Taste and adjust for seasoning.

Store in a glass jar for up to two weeks in the refrigerator.

▸ 1 clove garlic, minced
▸ 2 Tbsp (30 mL) Dijon mustard
▸ 2 Tbsp (30 mL) soy sauce
▸ 2 Tbsp (30 mL) rice vinegar
▸ 1 tsp (5 mL) freshly ground pepper
▸ ¾ cup (185 mL) grapeseed (or peanut) oil

Tarragon Port Sauce

An easy little sauce that packs a lot of flavor with a minimum amount of effort. What more could you ask for, other than reservations? It's perfect with grilled fish or barbecued chicken.

Makes ½ cup (125 mL)

Place the lime juice and port (or sherry) in a small stainless steel pot; bring to a boil and continue boiling until the liquid is reduced by half. Add the tarragon and remove the pot from the heat.

Whisk in the butter a cube at a time, taking care to whisk completely after each piece.

Add fleur de sel and pepper to taste. Serve warm.

▸ 2 Tbsp (30 mL) fresh lime juice
▸ ¼ cup (60 mL) port (or sweet sherry)
▸ 2 tsp (10 mL) dried tarragon
▸ ½ cup (125 mL) cold unsalted butter, cubed
▸ Fleur de sel
▸ Freshly ground pepper

Orange Beurre Blanc

David Long, the CEO of the prestigious Terminal City Club (in Vancouver), once stood in charge of their kitchen as executive chef. During his tenure, we did several charity events together, and this sauce was one of my favorites. It is perfect with grilled halibut, cod, and trout. Thanks, David!

Makes 1 cup (250 mL)

- ▸ 2 cups (500 mL) orange juice
- ▸ 3 Tbsp (45 mL) rice vinegar
- ▸ Pinch of chili flakes
- ▸ ½ cup (125 mL) cold unsalted butter, cut into small pieces
- ▸ Sea salt
- ▸ Freshly ground pepper

Place orange juice, vinegar, and chili flakes in a stainless steel pot and bring to a boil. Turn down the heat to maintain a slow boil and let the mixture reduce to a syrupy consistency. You will have approximately ⅔ cup (160 mL) remaining.

While the mixture is still hot, but not boiling, whisk in the cold butter pieces, allowing each addition to be absorbed before adding the next. Season with sea salt and pepper to taste. Pour over your grilled fish and serve at once.

Quick Hollandaise Sauce

Don't let the panic set in. Hollandaise in the blender is as easy as making a smoothie. Add finely chopped fresh herbs of your choice to switch it up. It's great with eggs, asparagus, and (real) crab.

Makes 1 cup (250 mL)

- ▸ 3 large egg yolks
- ▸ Juice of ½ lemon
- ▸ Pinch of sea salt
- ▸ ½ tsp (2 mL) ground white pepper
- ▸ 1 cup (250 mL) unsalted butter, melted and hot but not boiling

Combine the yolks, lemon juice, salt, and pepper in a blender. Whirl to combine. With the motor running on low speed, slowly pour in the hot butter. Be attentive—pour slowly and steadily with the machine running the entire time. Once all the butter has been added, the sauce should be thick and pale in color.

Miso Glaze

Simple, in one pot, and tasty: need we say more? Oh yes, it's great for basting salmon, mushrooms, or chicken.

Makes ⅔ cup (160 mL)

Place the vinegar, chili paste, ginger, garlic, and lemongrass in a small stainless steel pot. Bring to a boil, then turn the heat to a simmer, and reduce the liquid to half the original volume. Pour the contents through a fine-mesh strainer, discard the solids, and place the clear liquid back into the pot.

Whisk in the miso paste and soy sauce; let it simmer for about 5 minutes. To finish, stir in lime juice.

- 1 cup (250 mL) rice vinegar
- 2 Tbsp (30 mL) chili paste
- 2-inch (5 cm) piece fresh ginger, peeled and roughly chopped
- 2 cloves garlic, peeled and cut into quarters
- 1 stalk lemongrass (white part only), chopped
- ¼ cup (60 mL) miso paste
- 3 Tbsp (45 mL) soy sauce
- Juice of ½ lime

Balsamic Glaze

Here's a little secret recipe that chefs use to make the ordinary extraordinary, with a minimum of cost. Put the glaze into a squeeze bottle and use to garnish salads, grilled meats, and chicken—even ice cream. Balsamic glaze makes every home chef a culinary artist! Use plain, unaged balsamic vinegar (the inexpensive kind). A teaspoon (5 mL) of store-bought chili oil would give the glaze a little kick.

Makes a scant cup (250 mL)

Place the balsamic in a stainless steel pot over high heat. Bring to a rapid boil, turn the heat down to medium, and let the vinegar boil until reduced to a thick syrupy consistency. Add the corn syrup and cool.

- 2 cups (500 mL) balsamic vinegar
- 1 Tbsp (15 mL) corn syrup

Curry Sauce

Curry is my favorite sauce. It goes wonderfully with any fish and adds flavor and heat to stir-fries. This can be easily doubled up and frozen for future use. You can find concentrated chicken stock base, as a thick paste in jars, in gourmet food stores and many supermarkets.

Makes 2 cups (500 mL)

Melt the butter in a small heavy-bottomed pot over medium-low heat; add the shallots, garlic, and ginger. Sauté for about 2 minutes until the mixture is just soft. Stir in the curry powder, slowly whisk in the coconut milk, and increase the heat to medium-high. Add the chutney, chicken stock paste, and lemon juice. Whisk until combined. Reduce the heat to low and let simmer for 4 to 5 minutes.

- 3 Tbsp (45 mL) unsalted butter
- 2 medium shallots, finely diced
- 2 cloves garlic, minced
- 1-inch (2.5 cm) piece fresh ginger, peeled and grated
- 3 Tbsp (45 mL) good-quality curry powder
- One 14 oz (398 mL) can coconut milk
- 3 Tbsp (45 mL) chutney (any kind)
- 1 tsp (5 mL) concentrated chicken stock paste
- Juice of ½ lemon

IN A PINCH

This sauce keeps up to two months frozen, so make a double batch and keep it on hand when you're in a pinch for time.

Really Good and Easy Spaghetti Sauce

This makes enough for 1 lb (500 g) of dried pasta. I have premade bundles of bouquet garni in my pantry, and I usually just throw one in here if I don't have enough fresh herbs.

Makes 6 cups (1.5 L)

Heat 2 Tbsp (30 mL) of oil and the butter in a large saucepan over medium-high heat. Brown the beef and pork well; remove from the pan and set aside.

Add the remaining 2 Tbsp (30 mL) olive oil to the pan. Add the onion, carrot, and garlic and cook until soft and light brown. Add the tomatoes, parsley, bay leaves, thyme, and whole cloves and simmer for about 10 minutes.

Pour in the wine; add the undiluted stock paste and reserved meat and let the sauce simmer for about 1 hour with the lid on, adjusting the seasoning with salt and pepper to taste.

To serve, remove the sprigs of herbs and the cloves, add the fresh basil, and serve over hot pasta of your choice.

- 4 Tbsp (60 mL) olive oil, divided
- 2 Tbsp (30 mL) unsalted butter
- ¾ lb (375 g) ground beef
- 4 oz (125 g) ground pork
- 1 large onion, finely diced
- ½ carrot, finely diced
- 3 large cloves garlic, minced
- Two 28 oz (796 mL) cans San Marzano tomatoes
- ⅓ cup (80 mL) chopped parsley
- 2 bay leaves
- 3 large sprigs fresh thyme
- 2 whole cloves
- 1 cup (250 mL) red wine
- 2 Tbsp (30 mL) concentrated chicken stock paste
- Sea salt
- Freshly ground pepper
- 1 cup (250 mL) fresh basil leaves, chiffonade

15-Minute Gorgonzola Pasta Sauce

Four ingredients and 15 minutes is all it takes to make this savory Italian cheese sauce. This is great not only for pasta but also for dishes like the Rolled and Stuffed Chicken Breasts (page 98).

Makes about 1 cup (250 mL)

Heat the butter in a medium heavy-bottomed pot over medium heat; add the shallot and sauté for 1 minute. Pour in the chicken stock and boil over high heat until the sauce is reduced to ½ cup (125 mL).

Turn the heat to low and whisk in the Gorgonzola cheese. When the sauce is smooth and thick, pour over hot, cooked pasta and garnish with fresh Parmesan, pine nuts, and chopped parsley.

- 1 Tbsp (15 mL) unsalted butter
- 1 large shallot, minced
- 1 cup (250 mL) chicken stock
- 8 oz (250 g) Italian Gorgonzola cheese, crumbled
- ½ cup (125 mL) shaved Parmesan cheese (garnish for pasta)
- ½ cup (125 mL) toasted pine nuts (garnish for pasta)
- ⅓ cup (80 mL) chopped parsley (garnish for pasta)

Perfect Caramel Sauce

There are five undisputed dessert flavors that reign supreme: chocolate, vanilla, lemon, coffee, and, of course, caramel. This rich, delicious sauce makes everything taste better. The best pot to use is a copper sugar boiler from France. The pot is made of unlined copper, and it reaches extreme heats.

Makes 1½ cups (375 mL)

Combine the sugar, water, and lemon juice in a heavy-bottomed pot. Bring to a boil and continue to boil until the sugar begins to turn a light amber color. At this point, it darkens very quickly; watch it carefully so that it doesn't burn. The darker the color gets, the deeper the flavor becomes.

Slowly whisk in the cream. It will spit and spatter, so be careful. Cool to room temperature. Pour it on anything and everything.

- 2 cups (500 mL) sugar
- 2 Tbsp (30 mL) water
- 1 tsp (5 mL) fresh lemon juice
- 2 cups (500 mL) whipping cream, at room temperature

IN A PINCH

This sauce keeps up to 10 days in the fridge, so make a double batch and keep it on hand when you're in a pinch for time.

Hot Chocolate Sauce

This decadent chocolate sauce is as easy to make as opening a jar. You can make this sauce in advance—the morning of your dinner party—and then keep it in the refrigerator. Reheat just before serving. Good-quality chocolate will always list the amount of cocoa butter on the label—the higher the cocoa butter content, the smoother and richer the sauce.

Makes 1 scant cup (250 mL)

Place the cream, chocolate, and vanilla paste in a heavy-bottomed pot. Let the mixture simmer until the chocolate is almost melted. Remove from the heat and serve.

- ¾ cup (185 mL) half and half cream (10–12%)
- 4 oz (125 g) semisweet chocolate (a minimum of 50% cocoa butter), chopped
- 2 tsp (10 mL) vanilla paste

IN A PINCH

Add 2 to 3 Tbsp (30–45 mL) of your favorite liqueur or substitute ½ tsp (2 mL) almond extract for the vanilla paste.

11 Utensils I Can't Live Without

It's a question I'm often asked: if you could have only 10 utensils in your kitchen, what would they be? So here's my answer, except that it's a list of 11.

1 **Flexible plastic cutting board**

It follows you wherever the chopping job may be. I love the fact that you can pick it up easily, use it to transfer all the ingredients into the pan, and put it into the dishwasher to keep it food safe. These cutting boards are cheap and cheerful, so you can replace them frequently without feeling guilty.

2 **Messermeister peeler**

A great peeler that makes a mundane job not so mundane. It has a rubber grip handle with a serrated edge that will even allow you to peel a tomato if you get the urge.

3 **Instant-read thermometer**

This is an absolute must. No ifs, ands, or buts. Your food will be perfectly cooked and to a safe temperature every time. I prefer the digital readout over the dial, but then again, that's because my eyes seem to be letting me down on the hard-to-read things. Hate it when that happens!

4 **Microplane grater**

There was a time when grating cheese, citrus zest, ginger, or chocolate was a painful chore. The pedestrian, dull tin-box grater has happily been replaced with a razor-sharp Microplane. It cuts through blocks of cheddar in minutes, zest in seconds, and ginger without giving you the stringy bits. The edge is deadly sharp, so watch the fingers and nails.

5 **Mini sheet pan**

Finally, a baking sheet that has a built-in silicone finish—USA Pans. They have a characteristic ridged surface with a clear coating you can't see—and it's the best nonstick material. I love it for toasting nuts, oven-drying tomatoes, and even roasting chicken breasts. Cleanup is a breeze, and the pan is small and manageable.

6 Mini tongs

They act almost like an extension of your hand. I find that regular-length tongs give me hand cramps when I use them for any extended time. The mini tongs allow easy manipulation for the little things that are hard to turn.

7 Mock mandoline

A true, French-made mandoline prices out in excess of $275 depending on the brand. It takes most home cooks more time to assemble it than to slice anything with it. I love my inexpensive Japanese version. I use the thin slicer blade for potatoes, cucumbers, and radishes, but my favorite attachment is the julienne, which gives you the matchstick pieces in quick magical strokes. They are under $20, and the time saved is worth hundreds more.

8 Silicone basting brush

When I think of what could actually be lurking in those natural hair brushes, I close my eyes and shudder. A silicone brush is clean and safe. You can use the same brush for both sweet and savory because it washes really well. The silicone can tolerate thousands of washings and will not melt in the dishwasher or lose stray hairs in your food.

9 Silicone spoon

I am done with the burnt edges of wooden spoons. They look nasty, and the black cracked edges are eager to absorb bacteria. You can put the silicone spoon in the dishwasher, which makes it my stirring spoon of choice.

10 Peugeot pepper mill

I swear there is a pepper mill thief that infiltrates kitchens after dark and strips them of all working parts. It happens to everyone—the mill works fine during dinner one night, and the next day, it just ceases to grind. Ah, the ghosts of pepper mills past. My solution is to spend a bit more up front and purchase a grinder that comes with a lifetime guarantee—Peugeot is my choice. Problem solved!

11 Whisks

Cannot, would not, and will not live without at least three different sizes of whisks. They incorporate additions, inflate volume, and smooth out all the mistakes that a spoon makes. Whisk on!

Desserts

Coconut Macadamia Nut Cookies

A cookie with all the good things included.

Makes 2 to 3 dozen

Beat the butter, sugar, and vanilla together in a large bowl until light and fluffy, about 5 minutes. Beat in the egg and then stir in the flour, baking powder, chocolate, and macadamia nuts. Mix to combine well.

Divide the dough in half and roll each half into a round cylinder 2 to 3 inches (5–8 cm) thick, depending on how big you like your cookies. Lay a large sheet of waxed paper on your work surface, sprinkle the coconut on the paper, and roll the cookie cylinders evenly in the coconut. Wrap the cylinders in parchment paper or plastic wrap, and chill for 30 minutes.

Cut the cylinders into ½-inch (1 cm) discs and place on parchment-lined rimmed baking sheets.

Bake in a preheated 375°F (190°C) oven for about 15 minutes until cookies are golden in color.

- 1 cup (250 mL) unsalted butter, softened
- ¾ cup (185 mL) sugar
- 1 tsp (5 mL) pure vanilla extract
- 1 large egg, lightly beaten
- 2 cups (500 mL) unbleached all-purpose flour
- 1 tsp (5 mL) baking powder
- ¼ cup (60 mL) semisweet chocolate, chopped into fine pieces
- ½ cup (125 mL) chopped macadamia nuts
- ½ cup (125 mL) flaked unsweetened coconut

IN A PINCH

Once the batter is made, you can freeze individual logs and have fresh-baked cookies anytime you wish. Just thaw, slice, bake, and serve.

Sticky Fig Cakes
with Caramel Sauce

What can be said about dessert decadence!

Serves 8

Trim the stem of each fig and cut them into quarters. Place the figs and prunes in a stainless steel saucepan. Pour the water over them and bring to a boil. Cool slightly, then transfer to a food processor and purée; add the baking soda, pulse, and set aside.

Beat the butter and sugar in a medium bowl until mixture is light and creamy in color. Add the eggs one at a time, beating after each addition.

Stir together the flour, baking powder, and lemon zest in a small bowl. Pour the fig mixture along with the flour mixture into the bowl with the butter and eggs and stir well. Add the chopped chocolate and spoon the mixture into 4 oz (½ cup/125 mL) muffin pans. Bake in a preheated 325°F (160°C) oven for 25 minutes, until a toothpick inserted into the middle of a muffin comes out clean.

To serve, split the mini cakes in half, spread with whipped cream cheese (or mascarpone), and drizzle with caramel sauce.

- 1½ cups (375 mL) dried Black Mission figs
- ½ cup (125 mL) pitted dried prunes, chopped
- 1¼ cups (310 mL) water
- 1 tsp (5 mL) baking soda
- ⅔ cup (160 mL) unsalted butter, softened
- ¾ cup (185 mL) brown sugar, packed
- 2 large eggs
- 1 cup (250 mL) unbleached all-purpose flour
- 1½ tsp (7 mL) baking powder
- 1 tsp (5 mL) lemon zest
- 5 oz (150 g) semisweet chocolate (a minimum of 60% cocoa), chopped
- 1 cup (250 mL) cream cheese (or mascarpone), softened and whipped
- Perfect Caramel Sauce (page 162)

Really Quick Banana Bread

I thank Helen Redpath, Gourmet Warehouse's food manager, for passing this recipe on to me. I have lightened the quantity of sugar to compensate for using really brown bananas. The darker the skin on the banana, the sweeter the fruit is. This is a great way to use very ripe bananas.

Makes 1 loaf

Butter and flour a 9- × 5- × 3-inch (2 L) loaf pan. Tap out all the excess flour from the pan and set aside.

Sift the flour, baking powder, baking soda, and salt together in a large bowl.

Beat the eggs in a medium bowl; add the oil, sugar, mashed bananas, and vanilla. Beat well to combine.

Fold the banana mixture into the sifted flour mixture, ensuring that the ingredients are evenly combined. Pour into the prepared pan and bake in a preheated 350°F (180°C) oven for 45 to 50 minutes until a toothpick inserted into the middle of the loaf comes out clean.

Cool in the pan for 15 minutes, and then turn out onto a rack.

- 1¼ cups (310 mL) unbleached all-purpose flour
- 1 tsp (5 mL) baking powder
- 1 tsp (5 mL) baking soda
- Pinch of sea salt
- 2 large eggs, beaten
- ½ cup (125 mL) grapeseed oil
- ⅔ cup (160 mL) sugar
- 3 large, very ripe bananas, mashed
- 1 tsp (5 mL) pure vanilla extract

Mediterranean Almond Cake

Imagine a cake made entirely in the food processor. One bowl, no mess. To be honest, every time I make this cake, there is rarely a crumb left over. If there is, you can be sure there is a face-off in our house as to who gets it for breakfast.

Serves 10 to 12

For the amaretto cream, mix the mascarpone and liqueur together. Chill until serving.

Place the sugar and almond paste in the bowl of a food processor and pulse until it is crumbly. Add the butter and almond extract; continue to process until the mixture is creamy. Then add the eggs one at a time, pulsing after each addition.

Sift together the flour, baking powder, and salt. Add to the egg mixture. Pulse until a batter forms.

Pour the batter into a 12-inch (30 cm) round cake pan that has been lined with parchment paper. Tap the pan several times on the counter before placing in the oven. (This pushes the batter-trapped air bubbles to the surface, resulting in an even-textured, hole-free cake.)

Bake in a preheated 325°F (160°C) oven for 40 minutes until a toothpick inserted into the middle comes out clean. Invert the cake onto a large cake platter; let it cool.

Spread the toasted almonds over the top of the cake and lightly dust the top with a shake of icing sugar. Serve in wedges garnished with amaretto cream.

Equipment
- 12-inch (30 cm) round cake pan

Amaretto Cream
- 2 cups (500 mL) Italian mascarpone
- 3 Tbsp (45 mL) amaretto liqueur

Almond Cake
- 1 scant cup (250 mL) sugar
- ½ lb (250 g) almond paste (marzipan)
- 1 cup (250 mL) unsalted butter, softened
- ½ tsp (2 mL) pure almond extract
- 6 large eggs
- 1 cup (250 mL) unbleached all-purpose flour
- 1½ tsp (7 mL) baking powder
- Pinch of kosher salt
- 1 cup (250 mL) toasted flaked almonds (garnish)
- Icing sugar for dusting

IN A PINCH

Almond paste (or marzipan) is the miracle maker here. Buy it in the baking section, and keep several packages handy for those almond cake cravings that pop up now and again.

Use two 6-inch (15 cm) round cake pans if those are easier to find. (An 8-inch/20 cm pan will not work for this recipe.)

Zabaglione

In a traditional zabaglione, you use only three simple ingredients: fresh egg yolks, sugar, and Marsala wine. The proportions are usually one whole yolk to 1 Tbsp (15 mL) of sugar and 1 fluid ounce (2 Tbsp/30 mL) Marsala. If you like zabaglione less sweet, replace half of the Marsala called for with white wine. Using a copper bowl for zabaglione is ideal because the copper somehow coaxes the eggs to a larger volume. Similar results can be achieved using a simple stainless steel bowl set over a pot of boiling water. You just have to whisk a bit harder.

Serves 4

Place a copper or stainless steel bowl over a pan of boiling water. Continuously whisk yolks and sugar in the bowl until the mixture is thick. Slowly add the Marsala. The mixture will foam and thicken further.

Pour into serving dishes accompanied by fresh fruit of the season. Serve it warm rather than chilled and set—the flavor bursts out when served warm.

- ▸ 6 large egg yolks
- ▸ 6 Tbsp (90 mL) berry sugar
- ▸ 6 fl oz (¾ cup/180 mL) Marsala
- ▸ Fresh fruit of your choice

Mini Ice Cream
and Toasted Almond Tartuffi

They taste divine and they look perfect. Just use a silicone muffin pan, or silicone mini muffin pan if you want smaller portions.

Makes 6

Soften the ice cream just enough that it can be pushed into the silicone muffin cups. Fill the bottom half of six muffin cups with half the softened ice cream.

Top with 2 Tbsp (30 mL) of the crushed amaretti cookies and three or four of the brandied cherries (or fresh fruit). Top each of these with more ice cream, pushing down to seal the edges. Freeze the tray for 4 to 6 hours or overnight. The ice cream must be set.

Early the next day, place the toasted chopped almonds on a baking sheet. Release the ice cream balls (they will pop out easily) onto the tray of nuts. Roll the ice cream in the nuts, forming a nice ball shape. Be generous; coat them entirely, making sure you press hard so that the nuts adhere.

Transfer to a tray and refreeze until serving time. Serve with fruit or Perfect Caramel Sauce (page 162).

- ▸ 2 cups (500 mL) good-quality vanilla ice cream
- ▸ ¾ cup (185 mL) crumbled amaretti cookies
- ▸ ½ cup (125 mL) brandied cherries (or fresh fruit)
- ▸ 1 cup (250 mL) chopped toasted almonds

IN A PINCH

These perfect little dessert balls are ideal for making up to a week in advance of a party.

If you don't have a silicone muffin pan, just use a metal muffin pan and line it with plastic wrap. Remove the plastic wrap after chilling.

Apple Marzipan Puffs

A great little dessert made with prepared puff pastry, crisp apples, and marzipan. Try crowning this with a big dollop of crème fraîche or good-quality vanilla ice cream, while the dessert is still warm.

Makes 8

Roll the pastry out onto a lightly floured board, just slightly so that you get an even thickness. Cut it into eight 4-inch (10 cm) squares and place onto a parchment-lined baking sheet. Drop about 2 tsp (10 mL) of marzipan paste into the center of each pastry square. Sprinkle with one-eighth of the crushed amaretti cookies overtop.

Peel the apples, cut in half, and core. Thinly slice the apple halves and lay slices overtop of the amaretti (half an apple per puff). Sprinkle each with a teaspoon (5 mL) sugar.

Pinch the corners of the pastry together, encompassing the fruit. Combine egg with the 1 Tbsp (15 mL) water to make a glaze and brush on top of each pastry puff.

Chill in the refrigerator for 30 minutes. Bake in a preheated 400°F (200°C) oven for 15 to 20 minutes. Serve warm with a big dollop of crème fraîche (or vanilla ice cream).

- ▸ 1 sheet of frozen puff pastry, thawed
- ▸ 4 oz (125 g) marzipan (almond paste)
- ▸ 8 amaretti cookies (or soda crackers), crushed
- ▸ 4 Granny Smith apples
- ▸ 8 tsp (40 mL) berry sugar
- ▸ 1 egg, lightly beaten
- ▸ 1 Tbsp (15 mL) water
- ▸ 1 cup (250 mL) crème fraîche (or vanilla ice cream)

IN A PINCH

Italian amaretti cookies are small almond cookies that I use here to absorb the moisture of the apple. They work like sponges to suck up the moisture as the apple cooks. The pastry will remain crisp on the bottom with a lovely essence of almond.

If you do not have amaretti cookies, use one soda cracker on each puff. It will do the same job but without the hint of almond.

Frozen Marbled Chocolate Mousse

This is one of the easiest desserts in this book to prepare. It can be made up to a week in advance. For a party, use a shaped mold, something fanciful like a triangle, moon, or square.

Serves 6 to 8

For the white mousse, place the chocolate and milk in the top of a double boiler over medium heat. Stir until smooth and melted. Remove from the heat and whisk in the yolk. Set aside to cool.

Beat the white of the egg until stiff peaks form; set aside. Whip the cream until stiff. Gently fold together the cooled chocolate mixture, whipped cream, and egg white. Set this white mousse aside.

For the dark mousse, place the chocolate, butter, and water in the top of a double boiler over medium heat. Stir until smooth and melted. Remove from the heat and whisk in the egg yolks one at a time, mixing well after each addition.

Beat the egg whites until firm peaks form; set aside. Whip the cream until stiff.

Gently fold one-quarter of the beaten whites into the chocolate to lighten the mixture, and then gently fold in the remaining whites and whipped cream until the mousse is uniform in color.

Very gently swirl the two mousses together in a shallow dish lined with plastic wrap to create a marbling effect. Pour the marbled mousse into the prepared pan and freeze about 3 hours (or overnight) until set.

To serve, invert the frozen mousse onto a serving platter and slice into thin pieces and top with berries.

White Mousse
- 3 oz (90 g) white chocolate, chopped
- 3 Tbsp (45 mL) whole milk
- 1 egg, separated
- ½ cup (125 mL) whipping cream

Dark Mousse
- 4 oz (125 g) dark chocolate, chopped
- 1 Tbsp (15 mL) unsalted butter
- 2 Tbsp (30 mL) water
- 3 large eggs, separated
- ½ cup (125 mL) whipping cream

- 1 cup (250 mL) assorted fresh berries

Hazelnut Chocolate Pots

There have always been many different ways to make chocolate pots. This shortcut version uses a food processor. My version takes it one step richer by using a mixture of hazelnut chocolate, technically referred to as "gianduja" (pronounced *jon-doo-yah*), together with bittersweet chocolate. Hold on: if anything is great in small packages, then this dessert defines that phrase perfectly.

Serves 6

Place the chocolates in a food processor; process until mixture is almost fine.

Place the whipping cream and milk in a small stainless steel pot and bring to a slow simmer. Add the vanilla paste, hazelnut liqueur (if using), and ground cardamom.

Pour the hot milk mixture into the feed tube of the food processor, and let the machine run for about 20 seconds. While it is running, add the egg and run for a further 30 seconds.

Pour the mixture into little soufflé cups, espresso cups, or better yet, little pots de crème.

Chill in the refrigerator for at least 4 to 6 hours, or overnight.

To serve, remove from the refrigerator a half hour before serving. (Room temperature brings out the best in good chocolate.) Garnish with crushed amaretti cookies and a perfect fresh raspberry. Or top each pot with three pistachio nuts. I also like to garnish these with a little gold leaf foil or gold flakes.

- 2½ oz (75 g) gianduja (hazelnut chocolate)
- 4 oz (125 g) bitter or semisweet chocolate
- ¾ cup (185 mL) whipping cream
- ½ cup (125 mL) whole milk
- ½ tsp (2 mL) vanilla paste
- 1 Tbsp (15 mL) hazelnut liqueur (I like Frangelico) (optional)
- ½ tsp (2 mL) ground cardamom
- 1 large egg

Options for Garnish
- 6 amaretti cookies, crushed
- 6 fresh raspberries
- 18 whole toasted pistachio nuts or hazelnuts

IN A PINCH

Vanilla paste is a thick paste made from the seeds of the bean. It is used the same way extract is. The upside of using the paste is that you end up with flecks of vanilla.

Fresh Banana Ice Cream

Hold on to your Cuisinart! If there were one reason and one reason only to include this machine in your kitchen, this ice cream is it. It's magical—the frozen fruit whirling around while you pour in the cream transforms instantly into ice cream. You can scale it up or down with regards to richness: whole milk, half and half cream, or the whole hog with whipping cream. Whatever your choice, this is a slam-dunk dessert.

Note: Due to the lack of preservatives, this ice cream will not keep longer than four days. Don't worry — it won't last that long!

Makes 2 cups (500 mL)

- 4 very ripe (black) bananas
- 1 cup (250 mL) half and half cream (10–12%)
- ½ cup (125 mL) whipping cream
- 2 tsp (10 mL) vanilla paste
- 2–3 Tbsp (30–45 mL) hazelnut or amaretto liqueur (optional)

Peel the bananas and cut into 2-inch (5 cm) pieces. Arrange in a single layer on a tray and freeze for at least 3 hours until rock hard.

Combine the creams in a spouted measuring cup and keep in the refrigerator until ready. Once the banana is frozen solid, place the pieces into the bowl of a food processor.

Pulse 10 to 12 times to break up the frozen pieces—the consistency should be that of coarse cornmeal. With the machine running, slowly pour in the chilled cream mixture into the feed tub. Scrape down the sides of the bowl, and add the vanilla paste and liqueur (if using). Pulse a few more times to mix.

Serve immediately or cover well and freeze for up to four days.

IN A PINCH

Save up and freeze all those single bananas that turn dark and that no one wants to eat except for my mother! Cut them up and keep them in a container in the freezer. Then, when you're stuck for a dessert, you will amaze guests at what you can make in a pinch.

Barbecued Peaches

I enjoyed a version of these peaches at my dear friend Robert McCullough's house. The preparation is so easy. I have simply enhanced the filling with crushed amaretti cookies and the essential pantry must-have: caramel sauce.

Serves 4

Cut the peaches in half, pit, and places pieces on a rimmed tray.

Mix together the cheese, crushed cookies, and amaretto (if using). Spoon this mixture evenly into the peach cavities. Transfer the peaches directly onto a hot grill preheated to medium-high and close the lid.

Let the peaches cook for 5 to 8 minutes, until they are still firm but have a little give and the cheese has started to ooze.

Transfer to your serving plate and give the peaches a good drizzle of caramel sauce.

- ▸ 4 ripe but firm peaches
- ▸ 1 cup (250 mL) mascarpone cheese
- ▸ ⅔ cup (160 mL) crushed amaretti cookies
- ▸ 2 Tbsp (30 mL) amaretto liqueur (optional)
- ▸ Perfect Caramel Sauce (page 162)

IN A PINCH

If mascarpone (Italian cream cheese) is not available in your area, use ½ cup (125 mL) of regular cream cheese with ½ cup (125 mL) of ricotta. Place both cheeses in the bowl of your food processor. Whirl for about 10 pulses until smooth and creamy.

Fresh B.C. Blueberry Amaretti Crumble

Not every fruit crumble is created equal. My secret ingredient is Italian amaretti cookies. They not only provide the sponge to absorb the juices of the fruit so that the dessert does not become soupy, but they also release a lovely almond flavor that enhances this dessert perfectly. This is my son Jason's favorite dessert. What he doesn't polish off for dinner is ultimately consumed for breakfast—see ya later, Cheerios!

Serves 4 to 6

Combine all of the crumble ingredients together in a large bowl. Using your hands, mix well to form an even distribution of the ingredients. Set aside.

Put the blueberries into a 4 to 6 cup (1–1.5 L) shallow nonmetal baking dish. Mix in the crushed cookies. Top with the prepared crumble and bake in a preheated 350°F (180°C) oven for 20 to 30 minutes until the blueberries just begin to bubble and the crumble is golden brown. Remove and cool.

Dust with icing sugar and serve with your favorite decadent ice cream.

IN A PINCH

When blueberry season is over, substitute a combination of pears and apple. I use Bosc or Anjou pears and a Granny Smith apple. All you do is peel both fruits and cut into chunks. Strawberries and rhubarb make another great combination.

Amaretti Crumble

- 1⅓ cups (330 mL) rolled oats
- ½ cup (125 mL) packed brown sugar
- ½ cup (125 mL) crushed amaretti cookies
- ⅓ cup (80 mL) slivered almonds (optional)
- 2 Tbsp (30 mL) unbleached all-purpose flour
- ¾ cup (185 mL) unsalted butter, softened

- 4 cups (1 L) fresh local blueberries
- ⅓ cup (80 mL) crushed amaretti cookies
- Icing sugar for dusting

Fresh Fruits in Red Wine Sauce

My panic is never the dinner, ever…In a pinch, it is always the dessert. If you're the same way, maybe you end up purchasing dessert or eliminating it altogether, or opting for that lame standby, fruit and ice cream. But the thing is, quick dessert doesn't have to be lame! My girlfriend Diane Lawrence does it with scraped vanilla bean and Pinot Noir. Outrageously simple. Here is my version using vanilla paste and whatever red wine you have. I am counting on you to have a decent wine, not the boxed cheap crap no one wants to drink.

Serves 4 to 6

Heat the butter in a 10-inch (25 cm) frying pan over medium heat. When melted, add the sugar, and let it melt together and slightly caramelize, about 3 minutes. Add the vanilla paste and wine. Bring to a boil and reduce the mixture by a quarter. It should be slightly thick and syrupy.

Add the fruit and chili flakes (if using) and simmer on low for not more than 2 minutes, stirring to warm through.

To serve, divide equally into ice cream–filled bowls, and garnish with finely chopped basil and mint.

- 3 Tbsp (45 mL) unsalted butter
- ¼ cup (60 mL) berry sugar
- 1 Tbsp (15 mL) vanilla paste
- 1½ cups (375 mL) red wine
- 3 cups (750 mL) mixed fresh fruits (strawberries, blueberries, blackberries, cubed mango or papaya, or whatever your favorites are)
- Pinch of chili flakes (optional)
- 4 cups (1 L) really good-quality vanilla ice cream
- 2 Tbsp (30 mL) finely chopped fresh basil
- 2 Tbsp (30 mL) finely chopped fresh mint

Cherry and Hazelnut Chocolate Tart

I use brandied French cherries sold in a jar in this tart. You can also choose sour cherries if you like those better. The wow factor is the gold flake, although the shavings of white chocolate against the dark chocolate are usually sufficient.

Serves 8 to 10

Place all the pastry ingredients in the bowl of a food processor; pulse 10 times, and then let the machine run until the dough forms a ball on the side of the bowl. Wrap in plastic film and chill for 20 minutes.

When chilled, roll out the dough and fit into a 9-inch (23 cm) tart pan with a removable bottom. (If you find that the pastry breaks while rolling, simply press it into place. The dough is a short crust, so it will not be affected by overhandling like a flaky pastry would be.) Freeze for 15 minutes.

After freezing, line the tart with baking weights and bake in a preheated 400°F (200°C) oven for 12 to 15 minutes. Remove the weights and set aside.

To make the filling, heat the cream in a heavy-bottomed pot until it just begins to form bubbles. Turn off the heat, add the chopped chocolate, and whisk until the mixture is smooth. Cool to room temperature, but do not let the ganache set.

As soon as it is cool and still liquid, pour into the prepared tart shell. Scatter the cherries evenly over the chocolate and gently push them in so that they are covered. Chill the tart until it is set.

To serve, garnish with a swirl of white chocolate and gold leaf (if using).

Toasted Coconut Pastry

- 1 cup (250 mL) unbleached all-purpose flour
- ½ cup (125 mL) cold unsalted butter, cubed
- ¼ cup (60 mL) flaked coconut (sweetened or unsweetened)

- 1½ cups (375 mL) whipping cream
- 1¼ lb (625 g) gianduja (hazelnut chocolate), chopped
- 1 cup (250 mL) jarred brandied cherries, drained and halved
- 6 oz (175 g) white chocolate, shaved into swirls (garnish)
- Edible gold leaf (optional garnish)

IN A PINCH

I confess that to save time, I almost never fill a pastry shell with baking weights when I'm prebaking it. I find it easier just to take out the tart shell from the oven at the halfway mark and tamp down the parts that have puffed up. You can use a large metal spoon or a coffee tamper for this job.

Chocolate Coconut Cups

If you can melt chocolate, you can make this mini dessert. A silicone mold will help you look like a hero, but even that isn't necessary (see In a Pinch). Who can promise you the praise and accolades that only pastry chefs receive, with one simple little recipe? I can!

Serves 12

Melt the chocolate in the top of a double boiler; once the chocolate is smooth, add the coconut. Stir to combine so that the chocolate coats the coconut evenly.

Divide the chocolate mixture among the 12 cups of a mini silicone muffin mold. Using a small teaspoon, push the chocolate mixture into the cavity of the muffin cup. Press onto the sides to form a cup. Set aside until set or chill for 10 minutes to set quicker. To remove, simply peel back the silicone.

To serve, place the cups on a tray, fill with the lemon curd, and top with fresh berries.

- ½ lb (250 g) good-quality dark chocolate (a minimum of 60% cocoa), chopped
- 1 cup (250 mL) flaked coconut (sweetened or unsweetened)
- One 10 oz (300 g) jar lemon curd
- Fresh blueberries (or raspberries) (garnish)

IN A PINCH

If you do not have a silicone mini muffin mold, take a metal mini muffin or tartlette pan and line it with plastic wrap. Proceed as directed, pushing the chocolate mixture into the pan to form cups. Chill and remove. Peel the plastic wrap off and proceed.

Lemon Hazelnut Dacquoise

Light is never a word that associates itself with dessert. Until now. Egg white, a bit of sugar, and a mixture of lemon curd and cream ... Luscious, I say.

Serves 6

Place the hazelnuts (or almonds) on a small baking sheet; roast for 15 minutes in a preheated 275°F (140°C) oven. Remove and cool. Place the cooled nuts, along with half of the sugar, in the bowl of a food processor; pulse until the mixture is fine. Set aside.

Whisk the egg whites until stiff peaks form; slowly pour in the other half of the sugar and continue to whip some more. Add the vanilla and fold in the nut mixture.

Line two baking sheets with parchment paper. Draw six 3-inch (8 cm) circles onto the parchment on one pan. On the other pan, draw six 1-inch (2.5 cm) circles. Heap the egg white mixture into the circles, spreading to the edges while keeping the thickness even.

Place the pans into a preheated 300°F (150°C) oven for about 50 minutes. The circles will be light brown and firm around the edges. Remove and set aside to cool.

Set the individual circles on serving plates. Mix the whipped cream and lemon curd together. Spread some of this cream evenly onto the large cooled circles, and top with some of the sliced fruit and then the smaller Dacquoise disk. Spread with the remaining lemon curd cream and top with the last of the fruit. Dust with icing sugar and serve.

- ½ cup (125 mL) hazelnuts (or almonds)
- ¾ cup (185 mL) berry sugar
- 4 large egg whites
- 1 tsp (5 mL) pure vanilla extract
- 1 cup (250 mL) whipping cream, whipped
- ⅓ cup (80 mL) lemon curd
- 2 cups (500 mL) fresh fruit, strawberries, blackberries, kiwi, banana, etc., sliced if necessary
- Icing sugar for dusting

IN A PINCH

I never bother with removing the skin of the hazelnuts after roasting. They say to use a tea towel, but who wants hazelnut skins to get into the laundry and all of their clothes? If you prefer, just buy hazelnuts with the skin already removed.

Lemon Tart

A really good lemon tart usually takes the better part of an afternoon to prepare. This is my version, which uses a quality jarred lemon curd to shorten preparation by hours. (I like to use English Provender Lemon Curd. The Brits really know how to make a damn good lemon curd.) My dear friend Diane requests this tart every time she comes for dinner. Diane, you now have my secret!

Serves 8 to 10

Place butter cubes into the bowl of a food processor. Add the flour, icing sugar, and coconut (if using). Pulse the machine 10 times, and then let it run until the dough forms a ball in the bowl.

Remove the dough and press it evenly into an 11-inch (28 cm) fluted tart pan with a removable bottom. Freeze the unbaked shell for 30 minutes.

After freezing, bake the tart shell in a preheated 400°F (200°c) oven for 20 to 30 minutes until just barely golden. Remove and cool.

To make the filling, beat the cream and vanilla together until stiff. Add the yolks and beat 10 seconds, just until incorporated. Fold in the lemon curd until evenly combined.

Pour the filling into the cooled shell. Return to the oven and bake for an additional 25 minutes at 375°F (190°c).

Dust with icing sugar when completely cool and cut into wedges to serve. If fresh raspberries are available, they make a beautiful garnish around the edge of the tart.

Shortcrust Pastry

- ¾ cup (185 mL) very cold unsalted butter, cubed
- 1½ cups (375 mL) unbleached all-purpose flour
- 3 Tbsp (45 mL) icing sugar
- 3 Tbsp (45 mL) flaked coconut (sweetened or unsweetened) (optional)

- ¾ cup (185 mL) whipping cream
- 2 tsp (10 mL) vanilla paste
- 2 large egg yolks
- One 10 oz (300 g) jar lemon curd
- Icing sugar for dusting
- Fresh raspberries (optional garnish)

5 Quick & Easy Desserts

1 Custard-free brûlée

Mix one regular tub (which is about 2 cups/500 mL) of mascarpone cheese with the zest from half a lemon and ⅓ cup (80 mL) of sugar. Divide evenly into shallow ramekins. Top with sliced bananas. Liberally sprinkle the top of the bananas with berry sugar, and brûlée with a handheld torch.

2 Custom-made ice cream

Soften a container of good-quality vanilla ice cream. You want it soft enough to stir but not melted. Stir in ½ cup (125 mL) of Callebaut chocolate chips, ¼ cup (60 mL) toasted coconut (sweetened or unsweetened), a handful of fresh blueberries (if available), toasted nuts, Skor bar bits—you name it! Refreeze and scoop.

3 Gourmet chocolate bark

Melt semisweet chocolate in a small pot. Draw several 2-inch (5 cm) circles onto a sheet of parchment. Use the chocolate to fill the circles, keeping filling as round as possible. When the chocolate has cooled but is still a little bit tacky, top the circles with dried cranberries or blueberries, toasted pistachio nuts, or some orange rind. Use your imagination! Try toasted coconut, sprinkles, toffee bits, etc.

4 Grilled fruit

Skewer chunks of fruit—pineapple, strawberries, kiwi, and peaches all work great. Brush the fruit lightly with almond oil and grill on a hot barbecue for 2 to 3 minutes. (If you don't have almond oil, mix 1 tsp (5 mL) of almond or vanilla extract with ⅓ cup (80 mL) of grapeseed oil.) The fruit will soften and become golden. Serve with crème fraîche or ice cream. Easy!

5 Instant fancy sweets

Melt a good-quality dark chocolate in a small pot. Dip boxed shortbread cookies or rolled French ice cream cookies in the chocolate, then into any chopped nuts you have on hand.

Chili paste
Sisters Secret (Vancouver)
www.sisters-secret.com

Tapenades and preserves
Brickstone Fine Food (Quebec)
www.apgfinefoods.com

Citrus-infused olive oils
O (California)
www.ooliveoil.com

Curry powder
Monsoon Coast (Salt Spring Island, B.C.)
www.monsooncoast.com

Moroccan rub
NoMU (South Africa)
www.nomu.co.za

Cote d'Azur
(in-house brand of Gourmet Warehouse,
in Vancouver)
www.gourmetwarehouse.ca

Barbecue sauce
Chef Ann Kirsebom's Gourmet Sauces/BBQ Ltd.
(West Vancouver)
www.tequi-lime.com

Asian spice pastes, including Nasi Goreng
Asian Home Gourmet (Australia)
www.asianhomegourmet.com

Chicken and beef stock paste
Major (U.S.)
www.majorint.com/stockbase.asp

Wasabi mayonnaise
Cote d'Azur
www.gourmetwarehouse.ca

Indian candy
West Coast Select (Surrey, B.C.)
www.westcoastselect.ca

Flavored almonds
Nunes Farms (California)
www.nunesfarms.com

Lemon curd
English Provender (U.K.)
www.englishprovender.com/curds/

Chocolate
Callebaut (Belgium)
www.callebaut.com

Cacao Barry (France)
www.cacao-barry.com

Valrhona (France)
www.valrhona.com

Guittard (U.S.)
www.guittard.com

Acknowledgments

Where do I begin? To just say "thank you" always seems so, well, lame. But until the English language has a more meaningful way to express gratitude, "thank you" it is.

A book is coddled and nursed along by many people from inception to fruition. Authors can create recipes every which way to Sunday, but a publisher and the house he works for must believe in the project. They commit immense resources, both financial and personal, to the book. Naturally, my first and most profuse thanks go to Robert McCullough, my publisher. More importantly, he is one of my dearest and most treasured friends. Thank you to Michael Burch and Kristina Stosek, the owners of Whitecap Books, for their joint belief in this project and their willingness to commit to it. Thank you, thank you, thank you.

Photos make the food in the book real. Without them, the reader has to fly without radar. Hamid Attie, a seasoned professional photographer who has garnered numerous international awards, not only brought the recipes into living color, but he gave wings to this book. I think our week-long photo session was the very definition of having fun at work. We managed to pound out over 20 photos a day! Thank you for your calm and patience, Hamid, through the laughter and chaos. The girls welcome you into the DB club—keep that shutter clicking!

Thank you to "the A team": Doreen Corday, Rick Forde, Ruth Grierson, Diane Lawrence, and Susan Meister. They sautéed, boiled, steamed, fried, grilled, baked, chopped, rolled with wild abandon. They styled the photos with skilled experience, and they did it with plenty of laughter. Thank you all so very much for generously giving your time and expertise.

Special thanks to Melva McLean for her sharp pencil and skillful editing that made certain all of my recipes made perfect sense. Thank you to the girls at Whitecap: Taryn Boyd for her patience, guidance, and ability to calm me during the first round; Michelle Furbacher, for her incredible artistic talents; and Grace Yaginuma for her unfaltering detailed questions. And thank you to Ross Milne for the amazing design. Beautiful, it is!

Thank you to Ken Campbell, my computer superman, who, on more than one occasion, saved the day by rescuing vanished files. He even made last-minute house calls to calm my manic panic. I am, sadly, a true luddite! Ken: you are awesome.

Thank you to the fantastic team at the Gourmet Warehouse: Joyce, Kathleen, Helen, Norita, Jamie, Raj, Scott, Teresa, Leanna, Louise, Jim, James, Richard, Amarilde, and Maria. You are all wonderful and have truly been there through all the ups and downs. You hold down the fort every day, which makes it possible for me to do all the crazy things I do. Thank you all so much.

Many thanks to Brian and Tammi Kerzner for hosting the dinner (which is pictured in this book)! That would be the burnt chicken dinner. I hope it is the last thing I blacken without trying.

Thank you to my two best friends, Diane Lawrence and Susie Meister—you both know I place you on pedestals! I ♥ you both.

Lastly to my small but amazing family: my mom, Clara, my daughter, Christina, and my son, Jason. I love you more than Disneyland and diamond rings.

Index